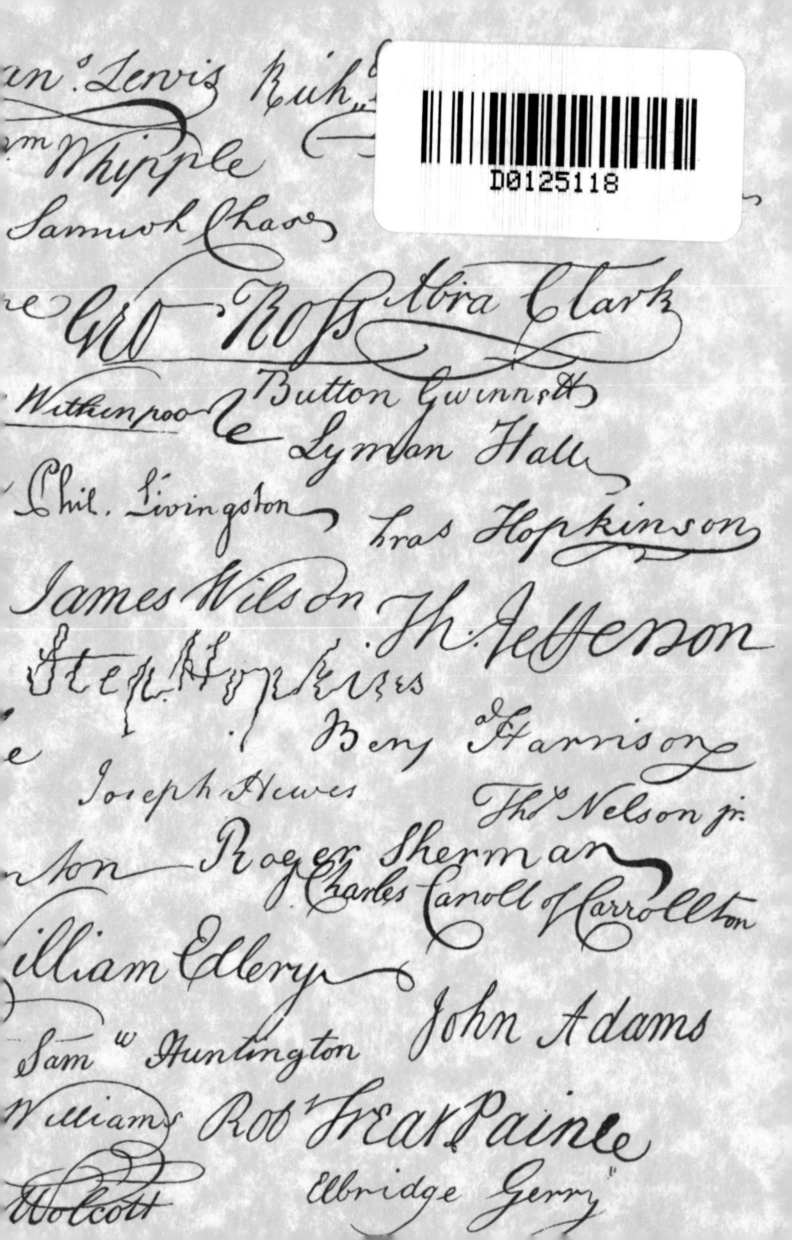
Whipple
Samuel Chase
Geo Ross
Abra Clark
Button Gwinnett
Lyman Hall
Phil. Livingston
Fras Hopkinson
James Wilson
Th. Jefferson
Step. Hopkins
Benja Harrison
Joseph Hewes
Thos Nelson jr.
Roger Sherman
Charles Carroll of Carrollton
William Ellery
John Adams
Saml Huntington
Robt Treat Paine
Elbridge Gerry
Wolcott

The

PORTABLE
PATRIOT

Documents, Speeches, and
Sermons That Compose
the American Soul

Edited by

JOEL J. MILLER & KRISTEN PARRISH

THOMAS NELSON
Since 1798

NASHVILLE   DALLAS   MEXICO CITY   RIO DE JANEIRO

Published in Nashville, Tennessee. Thomas Nelson is a registered trademark of Thomas Nelson, Inc.

Thomas Nelson, Inc., titles may be purchased in bulk for educational, business, fund-raising, or sales promotional use. For information, please e-mail SpecialMarkets@ThomasNelson.com.

Unless otherwise indicated, Scripture quotations are from the King James Version.

Library of Congress Cataloging-in-Publication Data

The portable patriot : documents, speeches, and sermons that compose the American soul / edited by Joel J. Miller and Kristen Parrish.
    p. cm.
  Includes bibliographical references and index.
  ISBN 978-1-59555-110-8
  1. United States—Politics and government—To 1775—Sources. 2. United States—Politics and government—1775–1783—Sources. 3. United States—Politics and government—1783–1809—Sources. 4. Patriotism—United States—History—Sources. 5. Speeches, addresses, etc., American. 6. Sermons, American. I. Miller, Joel, 1975– II. Parrish, Kristen.
  E173.P765 2010
  973.3—dc22

                            2010010627

Printed in the United States of America

20 21 22 WOR 10 9 8 7 6 5 4

It does not require a majority to prevail, but rather an irate, tireless minority keen to set brush fires in people's minds.

—Samuel Adams

Contents

Contents

INTRODUCTION

A PLACE, A PHILOSOPHY, AND A PEOPLE

The history of the first English settlements in America, and of the measures which prepared the way for a revolution in the colonies, is too interesting not to be well understood by men of common curiosity and reading. . . . That history unfolds a series of great events, evidently suited to accomplish important purposes in the economy of Divine Providence . . . events which every American of expanded views must contemplate with admiration; and every Christian, with delight.

—NOAH WEBSTER

We all recognize that America is a place. Most will recognize that it is also a philosophy. Say it, hear it, read it—however you encounter the word, America is inseparably attached to certain ideas and sentiments, values with which Americans generally identify.

Liberty, thrift, self-determination, public virtue, humility, courage, hard work, prayer, reliance on God—the American philosophy is a molten amalgam of the dreams and aspirations of millions of disparate peoples. But in our foundational years, perhaps more than many others, it was the master wordsmiths and orators, the pastors, lawyers, and politicians who forged and molded those values and hopes into solid prose and soliloquies. From the Puritans to the founders, the American soul was forged in the smithy of the spoken word and printed page.

We are a nation rooted in the revolutionary oratory of men like Patrick Henry and the pamphletry of Thomas Paine, the fiery rhetoric of Samuel Adams and stirring sermonizing from the pens and pulpits of men like the Revs. Samuel Sewell and Jonathan Mayhew. The colonial Committees of Correspondence and newspapers circulated revolutionary ideas, while incendiary tracts by James Otis and others gave backbone and resolve to the colonists. All the while Ben Franklin's wit shined and amused while it gave context and perspective.

Our reliance on the word goes back to the Pilgrims and the Mayflower Compact. It continues through the Declaration of Independence, the Articles of Confederation, the Constitution of the United States, and the Bill of Rights. It emerges in the political struggles of the Revolution and the ratification arguments of our national charter.

We find our identity in a mountain of words. *The Portable Patriot* mines that mountain and makes the choicest and most valuable selections from essays, extracts, sermons, poems, songs, and speeches available and accessible to a wide range of readers.

It should be noted here that we've abridged most of these selections from the originals. This book is a little library of foundational documents. To include all of these selections in their entirety would have resulted in a book considerably less portable. If you would like the unabridged selections, we've cited where they can be found. We've made some light edits for clarity but otherwise have left intact the idiosyncrasies of grammar and spelling common to the period.

WHAT'S BEHIND THIS COLLECTION?

Our motivation in assembling this collection is partly self-ish. As Noah Webster said, people "of common curiosity and reading" ought to know this story, and being commonly curious readers, we surmised that it couldn't hurt to improve our knowledge and appreciation of the American story. What better way than through its foundational documents and speeches? As Webster indicated, we discovered a great deal to admire, and as Christians we also found the delight that Webster said would accompany our contemplations. What else could we do but share what we'd found? Americans of any stripe should find passages that spark joy and stir the soul.

But more than our desire to learn and share, the balance of our motivation is to provoke. Our desire is to hold up the principles and values that make up the American philosophy and then pose a challenge, because America is not only a place on the map and collection of ideals. *America is also a people.* To say that America has its own peculiar philosophy is meaningless unless Americans act like it. Principles, philosophies, values, and virtues are all just empty abstractions until the moment that someone embodies them. We want to provoke more intentional embodiment of the ideals that compose the American soul—in ourselves and others.

Christians believe that the single most important fact in history is the Incarnation and the bodily ministry of Christ on earth, culminating in his death and resurrection. Far from a vague cloud of ideals floating in the ether, the Word became flesh. Jesus Christ had a ministry. He acted.

He served. This is the key to understanding such scriptural statements as "faith without works is dead" (James 2:26). To be real and meaningful, principles need bones and blood; they need hands and feet.

These are not merely things that people of "common curiosity and reading" should "contemplate with admiration" and "delight," though we believe these selections to be as enjoyable as they are edifying. But consider: These orators and writers lived real lives in function of their ideals. They labored, they struggled, they fought, some even gave their lives for the cause they upheld. Faith without works is dead, and politics without policies is a waste of time.

Our challenge comes in the form of a question:

If our selections reflect the American soul, what it really means to think, believe, and act like an American, then how do we measure up? It means nothing to have a heart swelling with patriotism if our hands are not manifesting the same.

Noah Webster gets at this point too. In his 1828 *American Dictionary*, he defines patriotism as "The passion which aims to serve one's country, either in defending it from invasion, or protecting its rights and maintaining its laws and institutions in vigor and purity. Patriotism is the characteristic of a good citizen, the noblest passion that animates a man in the character of a citizen." Passion and service. Ideas and action. Webster sees the connection plainly enough.

Do we?

I. Beginnings

―――――――

The stories of the early English settlers are a fascinating blend of trial and tribulation, prayer and steadfast hope, and their writings reflect it. The sense of promise and expectation flows through the lines of many writers from the time. The entries here are chosen to point to some themes that will feature throughout the foundational American experience.

The use of the adjective *foundational* is intentional. While it is a mistake to conflate the events from the days of English settlement with the founding period, they are undoubtedly linked. There are no discrete or mere facts in history. Everything is dependent on everything else because history is a web of related people, places, and events. We bear the stamp of those who came before us, and that was just as true for the founders as it was for us. The Pilgrims—and a host of other people who were long in the grave when the founders finally drafted the U.S. Constitution—played a vital role in the century and a half that followed because they helped shape the world that the founders inherited.

That fact seems obvious when you see the strong streak of independence that was manifest from the first and would eventually produce the rift between the Mother Country and her colonies, aspects that you'll see hinted at in these selections. It's also apparent in the assumed reliance on Providence and God's direction and help in the events unfolding at the time.

1. THE MAYFLOWER COMPACT

The Mayflower, a ship of 180 tons, set sail from England in 1620. Aboard were 102 souls determined to cross the Atlantic. After 63 stormy days, they landed at Plymouth, Massachusetts, where Plymouth Rock—a huge granite boulder—stood at the water's edge. These first settlers signed a covenant called the Mayflower Compact just days after they landed in their new home.

In the name of God, Amen! We whose names are underwritten, the loyal subjects of our dread sovereign Lord, King James, by the grace of God, of Great Britain, France and Ireland, King. Defender of the Faith, etc., have undertaken for the glory of God and the advancement of the Christian

THE MAYFLOWER. Image source: U.S. History Images, from *History of the Colonization of the United States,* by George Bancroft (New York: Julius Hart and Company, 1886).

faith, and honor of our King and Country, a voyage to plant the first colony in the northern parts of Virginia; Do by these Presents, solemnly and mutually, in the Presence of God and of one another covenant and combine ourselves together into a civil Body Politick for our better Ordering and Preservation, and Furtherence of the Ends aforesaid; and by Virtue hereof to enact, constitute and frame just and equal Laws, Ordinances, Acts, Constitutions, and Offices from time to time, as shall be thought most mete and convenient for the general Good of the Colony; unto which we promise all due Submission and Obedience. IN WITNESS WHEREOF we have hereunto subscribed our names, at Cape Cod, the 11th of November, in the year of the reign of our sovereign Lord, King James of England, France and Ireland, the Eighteenth, and of Scotland the fifty-fourth, Anno Domini 1620.

Mr. John Carver,
Mr. William Bradford,
Mr. Edward Winslow,
Mr. William Brewster,
   Isaac Allerton,
   Miles Standish,
   John Alden,
   John Turner,
   Francis Eaton,
   James Chilton,
   John Craxton,
   John Billington,
   Joses Fletcher,

Digery Priest,
Thomas Williams,
Gilbert Winslow,
Edmund Margesson,
Peter Brown,
Richard Britteridge,
George Soule,
Edward Tilly,
John Tilly,
Francis Cooke,
Thomas Rogers,
Thomas Tinker,
John Ridgdale,

John Goodman,

Mr. Samuel Fuller,

Mr. Christopher Martin,

Mr. William Mullins,

Mr. William White,

Mr. Richard Warren,

John Howland,

Mr. Steven Hopkins,

Edward Fuller,

Richard Clark,

Richard Gardiner,

Mr. John Allerton,

Thomas English,

Edward Doten,

Edward Liester.

The Federal and State Constitutions, Colonial Charters and Other Organic Laws of the United States, part 1, 2nd ed. (Washington: Government Printing Office, 1878).

2. MARY ROWLANDSON RECOUNTS HER CAPTIVITY

Mary Rowlandson was the wife of the pastor at Lancaster, Massachusetts, when she was taken captive by the Native Americans on February 10, 1675. For weeks Mary relied on the grace of God as she was forced to stay with the Indians as they fled through the wilderness to elude the colonial militia. On May 2, 1675, Rowlandson was ransomed for £20.

On the tenth of February 1675, Came the Indians with great numbers upon Lancaster: Their first coming was about Sun-rising; hearing the noise of some Guns, we looked out; several Houses were burning, and the Smoke ascending to Heaven. There were five persons taken in one house, the Father, and the Mother and a sucking Child they knockt on the head; the other two they took and carried away alive.

Their were two others, who being out of their Garison upon some occasion, were set upon; one was knockt on the head, the other escaped: Another their was who running along was shot and wounded, and fell down; he begged of them his life, promising them Money (as they told me) but they would not hearken to him but knockt him in head, and stript him naked, and split open his Bowels. Another seeing many of the Indians about his Barn, ventured and went out, but was quickly shot down. There were three others belonging to the same Garison who were killed; the Indians getting up upon the roof of the Barn, had advantage to shoot down upon them over their Fortification. Thus these murtherous wretches went on, burning, and destroying before them,

At length they came and beset our own house, and quickly it was the dolefullest day that ever mine eyes saw. The House stood upon the edg of a hill; some of the Indians got behind the hill, others into the Barn, and others behind any thing that could shelter them; from all which places they shot against the House, so that the Bullets seemed to fly like hail; and quickly they wounded one man among us, then another, and then a third, About two hours (according to my observation, in that amazing time) they had been about the house before they prevailed to fire it (which they did with Flax and Hemp, which they brought out of the Barn, and there being no defence about the House, only two Flankers at two opposite corners and one of them not finished) they fired it once and one ventured out and quenched it, but they quickly fired it again, and that took Now is the dreadfull hour come, that I have often heard of (in time of War, as it was the case of others) but now mine eyes see it. Some in our house were fighting for their lives, others wallowing in their blood, the House on fire over our heads, and the bloody Heathen ready to knock us on the head, if we stired out. Now might we hear Mothers & Children crying out for themselves, and one another, *Lord, what shall we do?* Then I took my Children (and one of my sisters, hers) to go forth and leave the house: but as soon as we came to the dore and appeared, the *Indians* shot so thick that the bulletts rattled against the House, as if one had taken an handfull of stones and threw them, so that we were fain to give back. We had six stout Dogs belonging to our Garrison, but none of them would stir, though another time, if any *Indian* had come to the door, they were ready to fly upon him and tear him down. The Lord hereby would make us the more to acknowledge his hand, and to see that our help is always in him. But out we must go, the fire increasing, and com-ing along behind us, roaring, and the *Indians* gaping before us with their Guns, Spears and Hatchets to devour us. No sooner were we out of the House, but my Brother in Law (being before wounded, in defending the house, in or near the throat) fell down dead, whereat the *Indians* scorn-fully shouted, and hallowed, and were presently upon him, stripping off his cloaths, the bulletts flying thick, one went through my side, and the same (as would seem) through the bowels and hand of my dear Child in my arms. One of my elder Sisters Children, named *William*, had then his Leg broken, which the *Indians* perceiving, they knockt him on head. Thus were we butchered by those merciless

Heathen, standing amazed, with the blood running down to our heels. My eldest Sister being yet in the House, and seeing those wofull sights, the Infidels haling Mothers one way, and Children another, and some wallowing in their blood: and her elder Son telling her that her Son *William* was dead, and my self was wounded, she said, And, *Lord, let me dy with them;* which was no sooner said, but she was struck with a Bullet, and fell down dead over the threshold. I hope she is reaping the fruit of her good labours, being faithfull to the service of God in her place. In her younger years she lay under much trouble upon spiritual accounts, till it pleased God to make that precious Scripture take hold of her heart, 2 *Cor. 12. 9. And he said unto me my Grace is sufficient for thee.* More then twenty years after I have heard her tell how sweet and comfortable that place was to her, But to return: The *Indians* laid hold of me, pulling me one way, and the Children another, and said, *Come go along with us;* I told them they would kill me: they answered, *If I were willing to go along with them they would not hurt me.*

Oh the dolefull sight that now was to behold at this House! *Come, behold the works of the Lord, what dissolations he has made in the Earth.* Of thirty seven persons who were in this one House, none escaped either present death, or a bitter captivity, save only one, who might say as he. *Job. 1.15. And I only am escaped alone to tell the News.* There were twelve killed, some shot, some stab'd with their Spears, some knock'd down with their Hatchets. When we are in prosperity, Oh the little that we think of such dreadfull sights, and to see our dear Friends, and Relations ly bleeding out their heart-blood upon the ground. There was one who was chopt into the head with a Hatchet, and stript naked, and yet was crawling up and down. It is a solemn sight to see so many Christians lying in their blood, some here, and some there, like a company of Sheep torn by Wolves. All of them stript naked by a company of hell-hounds, roaring, singing, ranting and insulting, as if they would have torn our very hearts out; yet the Lord by his Almighty power preserved a number of us from death, for there were twenty-four of us taken alive and carried Captive. . . .

Now away we must go with those Barbarous Creatures, with our bodies wounded and bleeding, and our hearts no less than our bodies. About a mile we went that night, up upon a hill within sight of the Town where they intended to lodge. There was hard by a vacant house (deserted by the English before, for fear of the *Indians)* I asked them whether I might not lodge in the house that night to which they answered, what will you love *English men* still? this was the dolefullest night that ever my eyes saw. Oh the roaring, and singing and danceing, and yelling of those black creatures in the night, which made the place a lively resemblance of hell And as miserable was the wast that was there made, of Horses, Cattle, Sheep, Swine, Calves, Lambs, Roasting Pigs, and Fowl [which they had plundered in the Town] some roasting, some lying and burning, and some boyling to feed our merciless Enemies; who were joyful enough though we were disconsolate To add to the dolefulness of the former day, and the dismalness of the present night: my thoughts ran upon my losses and sad bereaved condition. All was gone, my Husband gone (at least separated from me, he being in the Bay; and to add to my grief, the *Indians* told me they would kill him as he came homeward) my Children gone, my Relations and Friends gone, our House and home and all our comforts within door, and without, all was gone, (except my life) and I knew not but the next moment that might go too. There remained nothing to me but one poor wounded Babe, and it seemed at present worse than death that it was in such a pitiful condition, bespeaking, Compassion, and I had no refreshing for it, nor suitable things to revive it, Little do many think what is the savageness and bruitishness of this barbarous Enemy; even those that seem to profess more than others among them, when the *English* have fallen into their hands. . . .

But now, the next morning, I must turn my back upon the Town, and travel with them into the vast and desolate Wilderness, I knew not whither. It is not my tongue, or pen can express the sorrows of my heart, and bitterness of my spirit, that I had at this departure: but God was with me, in a wonderfull manner, carrying me along, and bearing up my spirit, that it did not quite fail One of the Indians carried my poor wounded Babe upon a horse, it went moaning all along I shall dy, I shall dy. I went on foot after it, with sorrow that cannot be exprest. At length I took it off the horse, and carried it in my armes till my strength failed, and I fell down with it: Then they set me upon a horse with my wounded Child in my lap, and there being no furniture upon the horse back; as we were going down a steep hill, we both fell over the horses head, at which they like inhumane creatures laught, and rejoyced to see it, though I thought we should there have ended our dayes, as overcome with so many difficulties. But the Lord renewed my strength still, and carried me along, that I might see more of his Power; yea, so much that I could never have thought of, had I not experienced it.

After this it quickly began to snow, and when night came on, they stopt: and now down I must sit in the snow, by a little fire, and a few boughs behind me, with my sick Child in my lap; and calling much for water, being now (through the wound) fallen into a violent Fever. My own wound also growing so stiff, that I could scarce sit down or rise up; yet so it must be, that I must sit all this cold winter night upon the cold snowy ground, with my sick Child in my armes, looking that every hour would be the last of its life; and having no Christian friend near me, either to comfort or help me. *Oh, I may see the wonderfull power of God, that my Spirit did not utterly sink under my affliction: still the Lord upheld me with his gracious and mercifull Spirit, and we were both alive to see the light of the next morning.* . . .

I can remember the time, when I used to sleep quietly without workings in my thoughts, whole nights together, but now it is otherwayes with me. When all are fast about me, and no eye open, but his who ever waketh, my thoughts are upon things past, upon the awfull dispensation of the Lord towards us; upon his wonderfull power and might, in carrying of us through so many difficulties, in returning us in safety, and suffering none to hurt us. I remember in the night season, how the other day I was in the midst of thousands of enemies, & nothing but death before me: It was then hard work to perswade my self, that ever I should be satisfied with bread again. But now we are fed with the finest of the Wheat, and, as I may say, *With honey out of the rock:* In stead of the Husk, we have the fatted Calf: The thoughts of these things in the particulars of them, and of the love and goodness of God towards us, make it true of me, what David said of himself, *Psal. 6. 5. I watered my Couch with my tears.* Oh! the wonderfull power of God that mine eyes have seen, affording matter enough for my thoughts to run in, that when others are sleeping mine eyes are weeping.

I have seen the extrem vanity of this World: One hour I have been in health, and wealth, wanting nothing: But the next hour in sickness and wounds, and death, having nothing but sorrow and affliction . . . .

The Lord hath shewed me the vanity of these outward things. That they are the *Vanity of vanities, and vexation of spirit;* that they are but a shadow, a blast, a bubble, and things of no continuance. That we must rely on God himself, and our whole dependence must be upon him. If trouble from smaller matters began to arise in me, I have something at hand to check myself with, and say, why am I troubled? It was but the other day that if I had had the world, I would have given it for my freedom, or to have been a Servant to a Christian. I have learned to look beyond present and smaller troubles, and to be quieted under them, as *Moses* said, *Exod. 14. 13. Stand still and see the salvation of the Lord.*

William B. Cairns, ed., *Selections from Early American Writers, 1607–1800* (Macmillan, 1909).

3. THE FIRST THANKSGIVING
PROCLAMATION, 1676

A common practice from the colonial days through those of the founding was to offer purposeful and public pronouncement of gratitude to God for his grace and provision—especially in the midst of trials. Early printed proclamations of thanksgiving were usually printed in broadside form.

At A Council,
Held at Charlestown, June the 20th, 1676

The holy God having by a long and Continued Series of his Afflictive dispensations in & by the present Warr with the Heathen Natives of this Land, written and brought to pass bitter things against his own Covenant people in this wilderness, yet so that we evidently discern that in the midst of his judgements he hath remembered mercy, having remembered his Footstool in the day of his sore displeasure against us for our sins, with many singular Intimations of his Fatherly Compassion, and regard: reserving many of our Towns from Desolation Threatened, and attempted by the Enemy, and giving us especially of late with our Confederates many signal Advantages against them, without such Disadvantage to our selves as formerly we have been sensible of, if it be of the Lords mercies that we are not consumed, It certainly bespeaks our positive Thankfulness, when our Enemies are in any measure disappointed or destroyed; and fearing the Lord should take notice under so many Intimations of his returning mercy, we should be found an Insensible people, as not standing before him with Thanksgiving, as well as lading him with our Complaints in the time of pressing Afflictions:

The COUNCIL have thought meet to appoint and set apart the 29th. day of this Instant June, as a day of Solemn Thanksgiving and praise to God for such his goodness and Favour, many Particulars of which mercy might be Instanced, but we doubt not those who are sensible of Gods Afflictions, have been as diligent to espy him returning to us; and that the Lord may behold us as a People offering praise and thereby glorifying him; The Council doth Commend it to the Respective Ministers, Elders and people of this Jurisdiction; Solemnly and seriously to keep the same. Beseeching that being perswaded by the mercies of God we may all, even this whole people offer up our Bodies and Souls as a living and Acceptable Service unto God by Jesus Christ.

—By the Council, Edward Rawson Secr.

"The Celebration of Thanksgiving Day," from the *Carnegie Library of Pittsburgh Monthly Bulletin*, vol. 26 (1921).

4. Edward Randolph's 1676 Report on New England's Disregard of Britain's Trade Laws

Edward Randolph was a British royal agent, a customs officer, and an American colonial official. His relationship with Massachusetts officials was less than friendly, and in 1676 he returned to England and filed a denunciatory report critical of

the colony's violations of imperial policy. The "act of naviga-
tion" referred to below is the Acts of Trade and Navigation that
governed commerce in all of the realm, including and especially
the colonies.

To the right honorable the Lords of his Majesties most honorable Privy Council appointed a committee for trade and
plantations.

An answer to severall heads of enquiry concerning the
present state of New-England.

[W]hat notice is taken of the act of navigation? . . .

The trade and navigation is carried on by a generall traf-
fick to most parts of Europe, as England, Scotland, Ireland,
Spain, France, Portugall, Holland, Canaries, and the Hans
townes, carrying to each place such commodities as are vendible, either of their own growth and manufacture or those
of the other plantations, and doe make their returns in such
goods as are necessary and vendible either in New England, or
in any other of his Majesties dominions in America; as brandy,
Canary, Spanish and French wines, bullion, salt, fruits, oyles,
silks, laces, linnen of all sorts, cloath, serges, bayes, kersies,
stockings, and many other commodities, which they distrib-
ute into all parts of the West-Indies; so that there is little left
for the merchants residing in England to import into any of
the plantations, those of New-England being able to afford
their goods much cheaper than such who pay the customes
and are laden in England. By which meanes this kingdome
hath lost the best part of the western trade, there being
very little exported hence but only such commodities as are

properly the product and manufacture of England and cannot be had in other parts. . . .

There is no notice taken of the act of navigation, plantation, or any other laws made in England for the regulation of trade. All nations having free liberty to come into their ports and vend their commodities, without any restraint; and in this as well as in other things, that government would make the world believe they are a free state and doe act in all matters accordingly, and doe presume to give passports to ships, not only belonging to that colony but also to England, without any regard to those rules prescribed by his Majestie.

Thomas Hutchinson, *The Hutchinson Papers*, vol. 2 (Albany: Publications of the Prince Society, 1865).

5. John Cotton on the Abuse of Power

John Cotton (1584–1652) was a Puritan leader who fled to New England in 1633. A well-respected theologian and preacher, he became a vital teacher in the Boston church. Here he wrote on the limitation of government. Going beyond the bounds God has set, said Cotton, is both injurious to the people and the leaders who expand the power given to them.

Let all the world learn to give mortal men no greater power than they are content they shall use—for use it they will. And unless they be better taught of God, they will use it ever and anon. . . .

It is therefore most wholesome for magistrates and officers in church and commonwealth never to affect more liberty and authority than will do them good, and the people good: for whatever transcendent power is given will certainly overrun those that give it and those that receive it. There is a strain in a man's heart that will sometime or other run out to excess, unless the Lord restrain it; but it is not good to venture it.

It is necessary, therefore, that all power that is on earth be limited, church-power or other. If there be power given to speak great things, then look for great blasphemies, look for a licentious abuse of it. . . .

It is therefore fit for every man to be studious of the bounds which the Lord hath set: and for the people, in whom fundamentally all power lies, to give as much power as God in His word gives to men. And it is meet that magistrates in the commonwealth, and so officers in churches, should desire to know the utmost bounds of their own power, and it is safe for both. All intrenchment upon the bounds which God hath not given, they are not enlargements, but burdens and snares; they will certainly lead the spirit of a man out of his way, sooner or later.

Perry Miller, ed., "Limitation of Government," in *The American Puritans: Their Prose and Poetry* (New York: Columbia University Press, 1982).

6. ANNE BRADSTREET'S "EPITAPH ON A PATRIOT"

Thomas Dudley, Esq., by many accounts was an obstinate man. His loving daughter, poet Anne Bradstreet (1612–1672), however, always spoke of him with tenderness. His death was a terrible loss for her. Her 1653 elegy on his death, including "His Epitaph," was full of her sorrow.

His Epitaph.

*Within this Tomb a Patriot lyes
That was both pious, just and wise,
To Truth a shield, to right a Wall,
To Sectaryes a whip and Maul,
A Magazine of History,
A Prizer of good Company
In manners pleasant and severe
The Good him lov'd, the bad did fear,
And when his time with years was spent
If some rejoyc'd, more did lament.*

John Harvard Ellis, ed., *The Works of Anne Bradstreet in Prose and Verse* (Cambridge: John Wilson and Son, 1867).

7. Epitaph of Benjamin Franklin, Written by Him in 1728

Not only did Benjamin Franklin sign both the Declaration of Independence and the Constitution, he was also a man of science, an author and printer, a consummate diplomat, and a philosopher. In 1728 Franklin wrote a premature epitaph for himself.

The Body
Of
Benjamin Franklin,
Printer,
(Like the cover of an old book,
Its contents torn out,
And stript of its lettering and gilding,)
Lies here, food for worms.
But the work shall not be lost,
For it will, as he believed, appear once more,
In a new and more elegant edition,
Revised and corrected
By
THE AUTHOR.

Jared Sparks, ed., From *The Works of Benjamin Franklin*, vol. 1 (London: Benjamin Franklin Stevens, 1882).

8. PETER KALM ON AMERICA'S LIKELY BREAK WITH ENGLAND

Peter Kalm was a Swedish-Finnish botanist and explorer who traveled throughout much of colonial America from 1748 to 1751, providing the first naturalist's description of such things as Niagara Falls. He wrote the observations and his prediction below in 1748, but his journals weren't published until 1773, just three years before America declared independence.

It is . . . of great advantage to the crown of England, that the North American colonies are near a country under the government of the French, like Canada. There is reason to believe that the King never was earnest in his attempts to expel the French from their possessions there; though it might have been done with little difficulty: for the English colonies in this part of the world have increased so much in their number of inhabitants, and in their riches, that they almost vie with Old England. Now in order to keep up the authority and trade of their mother country, and to answer several other purposes, they are forbid to establish new manufactures, which would turn to the disadvantage of British commerce: they are not allowed to dig for any gold or silver, unless they send them to England immediately: they have not the liberty of trading to any parts that do not belong to the British dominions, excepting some settled places; and foreign traders are not allowed to send their ships to them. These and some other restrictions, occasion the inhabitants of the English colonies to grow less tender for their mother country. This coldness is kept up by the many foreigners, such as Germans, Dutch, and French, settled here, and living among the English, who commonly have no particular attachment to Old England; add to this likewise, that many people can never be contented with their possessions, though they be ever so great, and will always be desirous of getting more, and of enjoying the pleasures which arises from changing; and their over great liberty, and their luxury, often lead them to licentiousness.

I have been told by Englishmen, and not only by such as were born in America, but even by such as came from Europe, that the English colonies in North America, in the space of thirty or fifty years, would be able to form a state by themselves, entirely independent on Old England. But as the whole country which lies along the sea-shore is unguarded, and on the land side is harrassed by the French in times of war, these dangerous neighbors are sufficient to prevent the connection of the colonies with their mother country from being quite broken off.

John Pinkerton, *A General Collection of the Best and Most Interesting Voyages and Travels in All Parts of the World*, vol. 13 (London: Longman, 1812).

II. Pre-Revolution

Despite the observations by men like naturalist Peter Kalm, the build-up to American independence was imperceptible to most. It came in little things, small antagonisms and discords that grew into riotous, fractious displays.

In some ways the groundwork had been laid in the previous centuries. When Rev. Jonathan Mayhew preached about the right of civil disobedience (item 1 below), he was working from foundations built by Huguenot and Puritan writers more than a century and a half before. All that was needed was reason to resist—something the British Crown and Parliament were soon to provide.

Following the French and Indian War, the imperial government was in bad financial straits. The taxes they attempted to raise in the colonies sparked the fights that eventually led to war.

1. Rev. Jonathan Mayhew Defends Civil Resistance

Jonathan Mayhew (1720–1766), a Congregational minister and distinguished Dudlein Lecturer at Harvard in 1765, preached this sermon on January 30, 1750, the anniversary of the death of Charles I. He was an influential participant in the early resistance to ecclesial and political encroachments of England.

A spirit of domination is always to be guarded against, both in church and state, even in times of apparent security. Civil tyranny is usually small in the beginning, like the drop in a bucket; till at length like a mighty torrent or the raging waves of the sea, it bears down all before it and deluges whole countries and empires. Thus it is, also, as to ecclesiastical tyranny—the most cruel, intolerant, and impious of any. From small beginnings it exalts itself above all which is called God and that is worshipped. People have no security against being unmercifully priest-ridden but by keeping all imperious bishops, and other clergymen who love to lord it over God's heritage, from getting their foot into the stirrups at all. For, let them be once fairly mounted, and their beasts, the laity, may flounce and prance about to no purpose; and they will at length be so jaded and hacked by these reverend jockeys that they will not even have spirit enough to complain that their backs are galled, or, like Balaam's ass, to rebuke the madness of the prophet.

Tyranny brings ignorance and brutality along with it. It degrades men from their just rank into the class of brutes. It damps their spirits. It suppresses arts. It extinguishes every spark of noble ardor and generosity in the breasts of those who are enslaved by it. There is nothing great or good where its influence reaches. It therefore becomes every lover of truth and of human kind, every true lover of God and of the Christian religion, to bear a part in opposing this hateful monster. And it was a desire to contribute a mite towards carrying on a defensive war against the common enemy that produced this discourse. . . .

The Christian precepts of forbearance and submission under private injuries are enjoined in more peremptory and absolute terms than any used which require submission to oppression and injustice in civil rulers. Any one may be defied to produce such strong expressions in favor of passive and tame submission to unjust and tyrannical rulers as are used by Christ to enforce submission to private wrongs. Yet few understand those expressions in a strict and literal sense. And the reason why they do not is because common sense shows they were not intended to be so understood. . . .

But it should be remembered that if the duty of universal obedience and non-resistance to a king or prince can be argued from Scripture, the same unlimited submission, under a republican or any other form of government, and even to all subordinate rulers in any particular state, can be proved by it as well; which is more than those who allege it for their own special purpose are willing to admit. The advocates for unlimited submission and non-resistance, if I mistake not, always speak with reference to kingly or monarchical government as distinguished from all others; and with reference to submitting to the will of the king in distinction from all other subordinate officers acting beyond their commission and the authority which they have received from the crown.

It is not pretended that any other persons, besides kings, have a divine right to do what they please, so that no one may resist them, without incurring the guilt of faction and rebellion. If any other secular powers oppress the people, it is generally allowed that the people may get redress by resistance, if other methods prove ineffectual. And if any officers in a kingly government go beyond the limits of the powers they have derived from the crown (the pretended source of all power and authority in the state), and attempt, illegally, to take away the lives or property of their fellow subjects, they may be resisted, at least till application can be made to the crown. But as to the sovereign himself, he may not be resisted in any case; nor any of his officers, while they confine themselves within the bounds which he has prescribed to them.

This, I think, is a true sketch of the principles of those who defend the doctrine of passive obedience and non-resistance. But there is nothing in Scripture which supports this scheme of political despotism or such arbitrary principles. The Apostle does not concern himself with the different forms of government. This he supposes to be left entirely to human prudence and discretion. Now, the consequence of this is, that unlimited and passive obedience is no more enjoined, in this passage, under monarchical government, or to the supreme power in a state, than under any other form of government.

The essence of government, I mean good government, and this is the government the Apostle treats of, consists in making good laws and in the wise and just execution of them—laws attempered to the common welfare of the governed. And if this be in fact done, it is evidently, in itself, a thing of no consequence what the particular form of government is; whether the legislative and executive power be lodged in one and the same person or in different persons; whether in one person, which is called a monarchy; whether in a few—whether in many, so as to constitute a republic; or in three co-ordinate branches, in such manner as to make the government partake of each of these forms, and to be, at the same time, essentially different from them all. If the end be attained, it is enough. But no form of government seems to be so unlikely to accomplish this end as absolute monarchy; nor is there any one which has so little pretence to a divine original, unless it be in this sense, that God first permitted it into, and thereby overturned, the commonwealth of Israel, as a curse or punishment on that people for their folly and wickedness particularly in desiring such a government.

If we calmly consider the nature of the thing itself, nothing can well be imagined more directly contrary to common sense than to suppose that millions of people should be subject to the arbitrary and precarious pleasure of a single man (who has, naturally, no superiority over them in point of authority), so that their estates and everything valuable in life, and even their lives also, shall be absolutely at his disposal if he happens to be wanton and capricious enough to demand them. What unprejudiced man can think that God made all to be thus subservient to the lawless pleasure and frenzy of one, so that it shall always be a sin to resist him.

Nothing but the most plain and express revelation from heaven could make a sober, impartial man believe such a monstrous, unaccountable doctrine; and, indeed, the thing itself appears so shocking, so out of all proportion, that it may be questioned whether all the miracles ever wrought could make it credible that such a doctrine came from God.

At present there is not a syllable in Scripture which gives any countenance to it. The hereditary, indefeasible, divine right of kings, and the doctrine of non-resistance which is built on the supposition of such a right, are altogether as fabulous and chimerical as transubstantiation or any of the most absurd reveries of ancient or modern visionaries. These notions are fetched neither from divine revelation nor from human reason; and if they are derived from neither of these sources it is not much matter whence they come or whither they go. Only it is a pity such doctrines should be propagated in society, to raise factions and rebellions, as we see they have, in fact, both in the last and present reign.

We may safely assert these two things, in general, without undermining civil government:—One is, that no civil rulers are to be obeyed when they enjoin things inconsistent with the word and commands of God. All disobedience in such case is lawful and glorious; particularly if people refuse to comply with any legal establishment of religion, because it is a gross perversion and corruption of a pure and divine religion brought from God to man by the Son of God himself, the only head of the Christian church. All commands running counter to the revealed will of God are null or void; and disobedience to them is not a crime, but a duty.

Mayo Williamson Hazeltine, ed., *Orations from Homer to William McKinley*, vol. 5 (New York: P.F. Collier and Son, 1902).

2. SAMUEL DAVIES'S "RELIGION AND PATRIOTISM THE CONSTITUENTS OF GOOD SOLDIERS"

In his brief life, Presbyterian preacher Samuel Davies's (1723–1761) fame as a preacher was so great that King George II invited him to preach in the royal chapel. Davies served the last eighteen months of his life as the president of Princeton. But perhaps his most dedicated ministry was during the years he preached in the backwoods of Virginia, where he welcomed large numbers of slaves to hear him speak. In this sermon delivered at the start of the French and Indian War in 1755, Davies rallied his listeners to arms against the French in the Ohio country.

"Be of good courage, and let us play the men" [2 Sam. 10:12]. Courage is an essential character of a good soldier—not a savage ferocious violence; not a fool-hardy insensibility of danger, or headstrong rashness to rush into it; not the fury of inflamed passions, broke loose from the government of reason; but calm, deliberate, rational courage; a steady, judicious, thoughtful fortitude; the courage of a man, and not of a tiger; such a temper as Addison ascribes with so much justice to the famous Marlborough and Eugene:—

> *Whose courage dwelt not in a troubled flood*
> *Of mounting spirits and fermenting blood;—But*
> *Lodg'd in the soul, with virtue over-ruled,*
> *inflamed by reason, and by reason cool'd.*
> —THE CAMPAIGN

This is true courage, and such as we ought all to cherish in the present dangerous conjuncture. This will render men vigilant and cautious against surprise, prudent and deliberate in concerting their measures, and steady and resolute in executing them. But without this they will fall into unsuspected dangers, which will strike them with wild consternation; they will meanly shun dangers that are surmountable, or precipitantly rush into those that are causeless, or evidently fatal, and throw away their lives in vain.

There are some men who naturally have this heroic turn of mind. The wise Creator has adapted the natural genius of mankind with a surprising and beautiful variety to the state in which they are placed in this world. To some he has given a turn for intellectual improvement, and the liberal arts and sciences; to others a genius for trade; to others a dexterity in mechanics, and the ruder arts, necessary for the support of human life: the generality of mankind may be capable of tolerable improvements in any of these; but it is only they whom the God of Nature has formed for them, that will shine in them; every man in his own province. And as God well knew what a world of degenerate, ambitious, and revengeful creatures this is; as he knew that innocence could not be protected, property and liberty secured, nor the lives of mankind preserved from the lawless hands of ambition, avarice, and tyranny, without the use of the sword; as he knew this would be the only method to preserve mankind from universal slavery; he has formed some men for this dreadful work, and fired them with a martial spirit, and a glorious love of danger. Such a spirit, though most pernicious when ungoverned by the rules of justice and benevolence to mankind, is a public blessing when rightly directed: such a spirit, under God, has often mortified the insolence of tyrants, checked the encroachments of arbitrary power, and delivered enslaved and ruined nations: it is as necessary in its place for our subsistence in such a world as this, as any of the gentler geniuses among mankind; and it is derived from the same divine original. He that winged the imagination of a Homer or a Milton; he that gave penetration to the mind of Newton; he that made Tubal-Cain an instructor of artificers in brass and iron [Gen. 4:22], and gave skill to Bezaleel and Aholiah in curious works nay, he that sent out Paul and his brethren to conquer the nations with the gentler weapons of plain truth, miracles, and the love of a crucified Savior; he, even that same gracious power, has formed and raised up an Alexander, a Julius Caesar, a [King] William [III], and a Marlborough, and inspired them with this enterprising, intrepid spirit; the two first to scourge a guilty world, and the two last to save nations on the brink of ruin. There is something glorious and inviting in danger to such noble minds; and their breasts beat with a generous ardor when it appears. . . .

What can do you a lasting injury while you have a reconciled God smiling upon you from on high, a peaceful conscience animating you from within, and a happy immortality just before you? sure you may bid defiance to dangers and death in their most shocking forms. You have answered the end of this life already by preparing for another; and how can you depart off this mortal stage more honorably, than in the cause of liberty, of religion, and your country? . . .

We fight for our people; and what endearments are included in that significant word! our liberty, our estates, our lives! our king, our fellow-subjects, our venerable fathers, our tender children, the wives of our bosom, our friends, the sharers of our souls, our posterity to the latest ages! and who would not use his sword with an exerted arm when these lie at stake? But even these are not all: we fight *for the cities of our God*. God has distinguished us with a religion from heaven; and hitherto we have enjoyed the quiet and unrestrained exercise of it: he has condescended to be a God to our nation, and to honor our cities with his gracious presence, and the institutions of his worship, the means to make us wise, good, and happy : but now these most invaluable blessings lie at stake; these are the prizes for which we contend; and must it not excite all our active powers to the highest pitch of exertion? Shall we tamely submit to idolatry and religious tyranny? No, God forbid; *let us play the men*, since we take up arms for our people, and the cities of our God.

I need not tell you how applicable this advice, thus paraphrased, is to the design of the present associated company. The equity of our cause is most evident. The Indian savages have certainly no right to murder our fellow-subjects, living quiet and inoffensive in their habitations; nor have the French any power to hound them out upon us, nor to invade the territories belonging to the British crown, and secured to it by the faith of treaties. This is a clear case: and it is equally clear that you are engaged in a cause of the utmost importance. To protect your brethren from the most bloody barbarities—to defend the territories of the best of kings against the oppression and tyranny of arbitrary power—to secure the inestimable blessings of liberty, British liberty, from the chains of French slavery. . . .

The consideration of the justice and importance of the cause may also encourage you to hope that the Lord of Hosts will espouse it, and render its guardians successful, and return them in safety to the arms of their longing friends. The event, however, is in his hands; and it is much better there than if it were in yours.

Albert Barnes, ed., *Sermons on Important Subjects, by the Reverend Samuel Davies, A.M.* (New York: Carter and Bros., 1849).

3. James Otis Opposes Arbitrary Law Enforcement

The Navigation Acts that the colonists so commonly flouted by smuggling were enforced by customs men who used search warrants called writs of assistance—overbroad warrants that allowed the government to search for smuggled goods practically whenever and wherever they chose and bring in the "assistance" of the sheriff to help in the effort. It's important to note that the smuggling was a response to legal impositions, including taxes, that the Americans opposed. In 1761, upon the ascension of King George III, new writs had to be issued, and lawyer James Otis took the job of opposing the issuance in the most famous legal proceeding of the day. He did not prevail, and the colonists found an early reason to begin the break with England.

May it please Your Honors, I was desired by one of the Court to look into the books, and consider the question now before them concerning writs of assistance. I have accordingly considered it, and now appear, not only in obedience to your order, but likewise in behalf of the inhabitants of this town, who have presented another petition, and out of regard to the liberties of the subject. And I take this opportunity to declare, that whether under a fee or not (for in such a cause as this I despise a fee) I will to my dying day oppose with all the powers and faculties God has given me, all such instruments of slavery on the one hand, and villainy on the other, as this writ of assistance is.

It appears to me the worst instrument of arbitrary power, the most destructive of English liberty and the fundamental principles of law, that ever was found in an English law-book. I must, therefore, beg your Honors' patience and attention to the whole range of an argument, that may perhaps appear uncommon in many things, as well as to points of learning that are more remote and unusual: that the whole tendency of my design may the more easily be perceived, the con-clusions better discerned, and the force of them be better felt. I shall not think much of my pains in this cause, as I engaged in it from principle. I was solicited to argue this case as Advocate-General; and because I would not, I have been charged with desertion from my office. To this charge I can give a very sufficient answer. I renounced that office, and I argue this cause, from the same principle; and I argue it with the greater pleasure, as it is in favor of British liberty, at a time when we hear the greatest monarch upon earth declar-ing from his throne that he glories in the name of Briton, and that the privileges of his people are dearer to him than the most valuable prerogatives of his crown; and as it is in oppo-sition to a kind of power, the exercise of which, in former periods of English history, cost one king of England his head, and another his throne. I have taken more pains in this cause than I ever will take again, although my engaging in this and another popular cause has raised much resentment. But I think I can sincerely declare that I cheerfully submit myself to every odious name for conscience' sake; and from my soul I despise all those whose guilt, malice, or folly has made them my foes. Let the consequences be what they will, I am determined to proceed. The only principles of public conduct that are worthy of a gentleman or a man are to sacrifice estate, ease, health, and applause, and even life, to the sacred calls of his country. These manly sentiments, in private life, make the good citizen; in public life, the patriot and the hero. I do not say that when brought to the test, I shall be invincible. I pray God I may never be brought to the melancholy trial; but if ever I should, it will be then known how far I can reduce to practice principles which I know to be founded in truth. In the meantime I will proceed to the subject of this writ.

In the first place, may it please your Honors, I will admit that writs of one kind may be legal; that is, special writs, directed to special officers, and to search certain houses, &c., specially set forth in the writ, may be granted by the Court of Exchequer at home, upon oath made before the Lord Treasurer by the person who asks it, that he suspects such goods to be concealed in those very places he desires to search. The act of 14 Charles II which Mr. Gridley mentions, proves this. And in this light the writ appears like a warrant from a Justice of the Peace to search for stolen goods. Your honors will find in the old books concerning the office of a justice of the peace, precedents of general warrants to search suspected houses. But in more modern books, you will find only special warrants to search such and such houses specially named, in which the complainant has before sworn that he suspects his goods are concealed; and you will find it adjudged that special warrants only are legal. In the same manner I rely on it, that the writ prayed for in this petition, being general, is illegal. It is a power that places the liberty of every man in the hands of every petty officer. I say I admit that special writs of assistance, to search special places, may be granted to certain persons on oath; but I deny that the writ now prayed for can be granted, for I beg leave to make some observations on the writ itself, before I proceed to other acts of Parliament. In the first place, the writ is universal, being directed "to all and singular Justices, Sheriffs, Constables, and all other officers and subjects;" so, that, in short, it is directed to every subject in the King's dominions. Every one with this writ may be a tyrant; if this commission be legal, a tyrant in a legal manner also may control, imprison, or murder anyone within the realm. In the next place, it is perpetual; there is no return. A man is accountable to no person for his doings. Every man may reign secure in his petty tyranny, and spread terror and desolation around him. In the third place, a person with this writ, in the daytime, may enter all houses, shops, etc., at will, and command all to assist him. Fourthly, by this writ, not only deputies, &c., but even their menial servants, are allowed to lord it over us. Now one of the most essential branches of English liberty is the freedom of one's house. A man's house is his castle; and whilst he is quiet, he is as well guarded as a prince in his castle. This writ, if it should be declared legal, would totally annihilate this privilege. Custom-house officers may enter our houses, when they please; we are commanded to permit their entry. Their menial servants may enter, may break locks, bars, and everything in their way; and whether they break through malice or revenge, no man, no court, can inquire. Bare suspicion without oath is sufficient. This wanton exercise of this power is not a chimerical suggestion of a heated brain. I will mention some facts. Mr. Pew had one of these writs, and when Mr. Ware succeeded him, he indorsed this writ over to Mr. Ware; so that these writs are negotiable from one officer to another; and so your Honors have no opportunity of judging the persons to whom this vast power is delegated. Another instance is this: Mr. Justice Walley had called this same Mr. Ware before him, by a constable, to answer for a breach of Sabbath-day acts, or that of profane swearing. As soon as he had finished, Mr. Ware asked him if he had done. He replied, Yes. Well, then, said Mr. Ware, I will show you a little of my power. I command you to permit me to search your house for uncustomed goods. And went on to search his house from the garret to the cellar; and then served the constable in the same manner. But to show another absurdity in this writ; if it should be established, I insist upon it, every person by the 14 Charles II. has this power as well as custom-house officers. The words are, "It shall be lawful for any person or persons authorized," etc. What a scene does this open! Every man, prompted by revenge, ill humor, or wantonness, to inspect the inside of his neighbor's house, may get a writ of assistance. Others will ask it from self-defense; one arbitrary exertion will provoke another, until society be involved in tumult and in blood.

Again, these writs are not returned. Writs in their nature are temporary things. When the purposes for which they are issued are answered, they exist no more; but these live forever; no one can be called to account. Thus reason and the constitution are both against this writ. Let us see what authority there is for it. Not more than one instance can be found of it in all our law-books; and that was in the zenith of arbitrary power, namely, in the reign of Charles II., when star-chamber powers were pushed to extremity by some ignorant clerk of the exchequer. But had this writ been in any book whatever, it would have been illegal. All precedents are under the control of the principles of law. Lord Talbot says it is better to observe these than any precedents, though in the House of Lords, the last resort of the subject. No Acts of Parliament can establish such a writ; though it should be made in the very words of the petition, it would be void. An act against the constitution is void, (vid. Viner.) But these prove no more than what I before observed, that special writs may be granted *on oath and probable suspicion*. The act of 7 and 8 William III. that the officers of the plantations shall have the same powers, &c., is confined to this sense; that an officer should show probable ground; should take his oath of it; should do this before a magistrate; and that such magistrate, if he think proper, should issue a special warrant to a constable to search the places. That of 6 Anne can prove no more.

Charles Francis Adams, ed. *The Works of John Adams*, vol. 2 (Boston: Little, Brown, 1865).

4. Benjamin Franklin's Advice on Becoming Wealthy

Benjamin Franklin's Poor Richard's Almanac *featured all sorts of practical and valuable information for its readers. At the time a rash of consumerism caused an overreliance on creditors and the financial ruination of many. Franklin addressed the concern with homespun wisdom about frugality and prudence that rivals that dispensed by the personal finance gurus of the present.*

Courteous Reader,

I have heard, that nothing gives an author so great pleasure as to find his works respectfully quoted by others. Judge, then, how much I must have been gratified by an incident I am going to relate to you. I stopped my horse lately, where a great number of people were collected at an auction of merchants' goods. The hour of the sale not being come, they were conversing on the badness of the times; and one of the company called to a plain clean old man with white locks, "Pray, *Father Abraham*, what think you of the times? Will not these heavy taxes quite ruin the country? How shall we ever be able to pay them? What would you advise us to?"—*Father Abraham* stood up, and replied, "If you would have my advice, I will give it you in short; *For a word to the wise is enough*, as *Poor Richard* says." They joined in desiring him to speak his mind, and gathering round him, he proceeded as follows:

"Friends," said he, "the taxes are indeed very heavy, and if those laid on by the government were the only ones we had to pay, we might more easily discharge them; but we have many others, and much more grievous to some of us. We are taxed twice as much by our idleness, three times as much by our pride, and four times as much by our folly; and from these taxes the commissioners cannot ease or deliver us, by allowing an abatement. However, let us hearken to good advice, and something may be done for us; *God helps them that help themselves*, as *Poor Richard* says.

"I. It would be thought a hard government that should tax its people one-tenth part of their time, to be employed in its service: but idleness taxes many of us much more; sloth, by bringing on diseases, absolutely shortens life. *Sloth, like rust, consumes faster than labor wears; while the used key is always bright,* as *Poor Richard* says. *But dost thou love life, then do not squander time, for that is the stuff life is made of,* as *Poor Richard* says. How much more than is necessary do we spend in sleep! forgetting, that *The sleeping fox catches no poultry, and that there will be sleeping enough in the grave,* as *Poor Richard* says.

"*If time be of all things the most precious, wasting time must be,* as *Poor Richard* says, *the greatest prodigality;* since, as he elsewhere tells us, *Lost time is never found again; and what we call time enough, always proves little enough:* let us then up and be doing, and doing to the purpose; so by diligence shall we do more with less perplexity. *Sloth makes all things difficult, but industry all easy; and he that riseth late must trot all day, and shall scarce overtake his business at night; while laziness travels so slowly, that poverty soon overtakes him. Drive thy business, let not that drive thee; and early to bed, and early to rise, makes a man healthy, wealthy, and wise,* as *Poor Richard* says.

"So what signifies wishing and hoping for better times? We may make these times better if we bestir ourselves. *Industry need not wish, and he that lives upon hopes will die fasting. There are no gains without pains; then help hands, for I have no lands;* or, if I have, they are smartly taxed. *He that hath a trade, hath an estate; and he that hath a calling, hath an office of profit and honor,* as *Poor Richard* says; but then the trade must be worked at, and the calling followed, or neither the estate nor the office will enable us to pay our taxes. If we are industrious we shall never starve; for, *At the working man's house, hunger looks in, but dares not enter.* Nor will the bailiff or the constable enter, for *Industry pays debts, while despair increaseth them.* What though you have found no treasure, nor has any rich relation left you a legacy, *Diligence is the mother of good luck, and God gives all things to industry. Then plough deep, while sluggards sleep, and you shall have corn to sell and to keep.* Work while it is called to-day, for you know not how much you may be hindered to-morrow. *One to-day is worth two to-morrows,* as *Poor Richard* says; and further, *Never leave that till to-morrow which you can do to-day.* If you were a servant, would you not be ashamed that a good master should catch you idle? Are you then your own master? be ashamed to catch yourself idle, when there is so much to be done for yourself, your family, your country, and your king. Handle your tools without mittens; remember that *The cat in gloves catches no mice,* as *Poor Richard* says. It is true there is much to be done, and perhaps you are weak-handed; but stick to it steadily, and you will see great effects; for *Constant dropping wears away stones; and by diligence and patience the mouse ate in two the cable; and little strokes fell great oaks.*

"Methinks I hear some of you say, 'Must a man afford himself no leisure?'—I will tell thee, my friend, what *Poor Richard* says, *Employ thy time well, if thou meanest to gain leisure; and since thou art not sure of a minute, throw not away an hour.* Leisure is time for doing something useful; this leisure the diligent man will obtain, but the lazy man never; for, *A life of leisure and a life of laziness are two things. Many, without labor, would live by their wits only, but they break for want of stock;* whereas industry gives comfort, and plenty, and respect. *Fly pleasures, and they will follow you. The diligent spinner has a large shift; and now I have a sheep and a cow, every body bids me good morrow.*

"II. But with our industry we must likewise be steady, settled, and careful, and oversee our own affairs with our own eyes, and not trust too much to others; for, as *Poor Richard* says,

> *I never saw an oft-removed tree,*
> *Nor yet an oft-removed family,*
> *That throve so well as those that settled be.*

And again, *Three removes are as bad as a fire;* and again, *Keep thy shop, and thy shop will keep thee;* and again, *If you would have your business done, go; if not, send.* And again,

> *He that by the plough would thrive,*
> *Himself must either hold or drive.*

And again, *The eye of a master will do more work than both his hands*; and again, *Want of care does us more damage than want of knowledge*; and again, *Not to oversee workmen, is to leave them your purse open.* Trusting too much to others' care is the ruin of many; for, *In the affairs of this world men are saved, not by faith, but by the want of it*; but a man's own care is profitable; for, *If you would have a faithful servant, and one that you like, serve yourself. A little neglect may breed great mischief: for want of a nail the shoe was lost; for want of a shoe the horse was lost; and for want of a horse the rider was lost, being overtaken and slain by the enemy; all for want of a little care about a horse-shoe nail.*

"III. So much for industry, my friends, and attention to one's own business; but to these we must add frugality, if we would make our industry more certainly successful. A man may, if he knows not how to save as he gets, keep his nose all his life to the grindstone, and die not worth a groat at last. *A fat kitchen makes a lean will*; and,

> *Many estates are spent in the getting,*
> *Since women for tea forsook spinning and knitting,*
> *And men for punch forsook hewing and splitting.*

> *If you would be wealthy, think of saving as well as of getting. The Indies have not made Spain rich, because her outgoes are greater than her incomes.*

"Away then with your expensive follies, and you will not then have so much cause to complain of hard times, heavy taxes, and chargeable families; for

Women and wine, game and deceit,
Make the wealth small and the want great.

And further, *What maintains one vice, would bring up two children.* You may think, perhaps, that a little tea, or a little punch now and then, diet a little more costly, clothes a little finer, and a little entertainment now and then, can be no great matter; but remember, *Many a little makes a mickle.* Beware of little expenses; *A small leak will sink a great ship*, as *Poor Richard* says; and again, *Who dainties love, shall beggars prove*; and moreover, *Fools make feasts, and wise men eat them.*

"Here you are all got together at this sale of fineries and nick-nacks. You call them *goods*; but, if you do not take care, they will prove *evils* to some of you. You expect they will be sold cheap, and perhaps they may for less than they cost; but, if you have no occasion for them, they must be dear to you. Remember what *Poor Richard* says, *Buy what thou hast no need of, and ere long thou shalt sell thy necessaries.* And again, *At a great pennyworth pause a while.* He means, that perhaps the cheapness is apparent only, and not real; or the bargain, by straitening thee in thy business, may do thee more harm than good. For in another place he says, *Many have been ruined by buying good pennyworths.* Again, *It is foolish to lay out money in a purchase of repentance*; and yet this folly is practised every day at auctions, for want of minding the Almanack. Many a one, for the sake of finery on the back, have gone with a hungry belly and half-starved their families: *Silks and satins, scarlet and velvets, put out the kitchen fire*, as *Poor Richard* says.

These are not the necessaries of life; they can scarcely be called the conveniences; and yet, only because they look pretty, how many want to have them! By these, and other extravagancies, the genteel are reduced to poverty, and forced to borrow of those whom they formerly despised, but who, through industry and frugality, have maintained their standing; in which case it appears plainly, that, *A ploughman on his legs is higher than a gentleman on his knees*, as *Poor Richard* says. Perhaps they have had a small estate left them, which they knew not the getting of; they think *It is day, and will never be night*; that a little to be spent out of so much is not worth minding; but *Always taking out of the meal-tub, and never putting in, soon comes to the bottom*, as *Poor Richard* says; and then, *When the well is dry, they know the worth of water*. But this they might have known before, if they had taken his advice:—*If you would know the value of money, go and try to borrow some; for he that goes a borrowing goes a sorrowing*, as *Poor Richard* says; and indeed so does he that lends to such people, when he goes to get it in again.—*Poor Dick* further advises, and says,

> *Fond pride of dress is sure a very curse;*
> *Ere fancy you consult, consult your purse.*

And again, *Pride is as loud a beggar as Want, and a great deal more saucy*. When you have bought one fine thing, you must buy ten more, that your appearance may be all of a piece; but *Poor Dick* says, *It is easier to suppress the first desire, than to satisfy all that follow it*. And it is as truly folly for the poor to ape the rich, as for the frog to swell in order to equal the ox.

Vessels large may venture more,
But little boats should keep near shore.

It is, however, a folly soon punished; for, as *Poor Richard* says, *Pride that dines on vanity, sups on contempt; Pride breakfasted with Plenty, dined with Poverty, and supped with Infamy.* And, after all, of what use is this pride of appearance, for which so much is risked, so much is suffered? It cannot promote health, nor ease pain; it makes no increase of merit in the person; it creates envy; it hastens misfortune.

"But what madness must it be to *run in debt* for these superfluities? We are offered by the terms of this sale, six months' credit; and that, perhaps, has induced some of us to attend it, because we cannot spare the ready money, and hope now to be fine without it. But, ah! think what you do when you run in debt; you give to another power over your liberty. If you cannot pay at the time, you will be ashamed to see your creditor; you will be in fear when you speak to him; you will make poor pitiful sneaking excuses, and, by degrees, come to lose your veracity, and sink into base downright lying; for, *The second vice is lying, the first is running in debt,* as *Poor Richard* says; and again, to the same purpose, *Lying rides upon Debt's back:* whereas a free-born Englishman ought not to be ashamed nor afraid to see or speak to any man living. But poverty often deprives a man of all spirit and virtue. It *is hard for an empty bag to stand upright.* What would you think of that prince, or of that government, who should issue an edict forbidding you to dress like a gentleman or gentlewoman, on pain of imprisonment or servitude? Would you not say that you were free, have a right to dress as you please, and that such an edict would be a breach of your privileges, and such a government tyrannical? And yet you are about to put yourself under such tyranny, when you run in debt for such dress! Your creditor has authority, at his pleasure, to deprive you of your liberty, by confining you in gaol till you shall be able to pay him. When you have got your bargain, you may, perhaps, think little of payment; but, as *Poor Richard* says, *Creditors have better memories than debtors; creditors are a superstitious sect, great observers of set days and times.* The day comes round before you are aware, and the demand is made before you are prepared to satisfy it; or, if you bear your debt in mind, the term, which at first seemed so long, will, as it lessens, appear extremely short: time will seem to have added wings to his heels as well as his shoulders. *Those have a short Lent, who owe money to be paid at Easter.* At present, perhaps, you may think yourselves in thriving circumstances, and that you can bear a little extravagance without injury; but

> *For age and want save while you may,*
> *No morning sun lasts a whole day.*

Gain may be temporary and uncertain, but ever, while you live, expense is constant and certain; and, *It is easier to build two chimnies, than to keep one in fuel,* as *Poor Richard* says: so, rather go to bed supperless, than rise in debt.

> *Get what you can, and what you get hold:*
> *'Tis the stone that will turn all your lead into gold.*

And, when you have got the philosopher's stone, sure you will no longer complain of bad times, or the difficulty of paying taxes.

"IV. This doctrine, my friends, is reason and wisdom: but, after all, do not depend too much upon your own industry, and frugality, and prudence, though excellent things; for they may all be blasted, without the blessing of Heaven; and, therefore, ask that blessing humbly, and be not uncharitable to those that at present seem to want it, but comfort and help them. Remember, Job suffered, and was afterwards prosperous.

"And now, to conclude, *Experience keeps a dear school, but fools will learn in no other,* as *Poor Richard* says, and scarce in that; for, it is true, *We may give advice, but we cannot give conduct.* However, remember this, *They that will not be counselled, cannot be helped;* and further, that *If you will not hear Reason, she will surely rap your knuckles,* as *Poor Richard* says.

Thus the old gentleman ended his harangue. The people heard it and approved the doctrine; and immediately practised the contrary, just as if it had been a common sermon; for the auction opened, and they began to buy extravagantly.—I found the good man had thoroughly studied my almanacks, and digested all I had dropt on these topics during the course of twenty-five years. The frequent mention he made of me must have tired any one else; but my vanity was wonderfully delighted with it, though I was conscious that not a tenth part of the wisdom was my own which he ascribed to me, but rather the gleanings that I had made of the sense of all ages and nations. However, I resolved to be the better for the echo of it; and, though I had at first determined to buy stuff for a new coat, I went away resolved to wear my old one a little longer. Reader, if thou wilt do the same, thy profit will be as great as mine. I am, as ever, thine to serve thee,

—RICHARD SAUNDERS

Benjamin Franklin, *Memoirs of the Life and Writings of Benjamin Franklin*, vol. 5, 3rd ed. (London: Henry Colburn, 1819).

BENJAMIN FRANKLIN. Image source: U.S. Library of Congress. Portrait by Johann Elias Haid (1739–1809), engraver.

5. BENJAMIN FRANKLIN'S CATECHISM ON NATIONAL DEBT

Poor Richard's advice in the previous selection is ignored by no one as much as governments; witness today's U.S. federal debt, if no other examples flash readily to mind. Thankfully, Benjamin Franklin also took a jab at the bad financial habits of magistrates, though his conclusion is less than hopeful.

QUESTION 1. Supposing this debt to be only 195 millions of pounds sterling at present,* although it is much more, and that was all to be counted in shillings, that a man could count at the rate of 100 shillings per minute, for 12 hours each day, till he has counted the whole, how long would he take in doing it?

ANSWER. One hundred forty-eight years, one hundred nine days, and twenty-two hours.

Q. 2. The whole of this sum being 3,900 millions of shillings, and the coinage standard being sixty-two in the troy pound [the common measurement for fine metals], what is the whole weight of this sum?

A. Sixty-one millions, seven hundred fifty-two thousand, four hundred and seventy-six troy pounds.

Q. 3. How many ships would carry this weight, suppose 100 tons each?

A. Three hundred and fourteen ships.

Q. 4. How many carts would carry this weight, suppose a ton in each?

A. Thirty-one thousand, four hundred and fifty-two carts.

Q. 5. The breadth of a shilling being one inch, if all these shillings were laid in a straight line, close to one another's edges, how long would that line be that would contain them?

A. Sixty-one thousand, five hundred fifty-two miles; which is 9,572 miles more than twice round the whole circumference of the earth.

---

* At present (1777) it is said to be at least 230 millions.

THE STAMP ACT. Image source: U.S. History Images, from *Colonial Days: Being Stories and Ballads for Young Patriots*, by Richard Markham (New York: Dodd, Mead, & Company, 1881).

Q. 6. Suppose the interest of this debt to be three and a half per cent. per annum, what does the whole annual interest amount to?

A. Six millions, seven hundred and seventy thousand pounds.

Q. 7. How doth government raise this interest annually?

A. By taxing those who lent the principal, and others.

Q. 8. When will government be able to pay the principal?

A. When there is more money in England's treasury than there is in all Europe.

Q. 9. And when will that be?

A. Never.

Benjamin Franklin, *Memoirs of the Life and Writings of Benjamin Franklin*, vol. 5, 3rd ed. (London: Henry Colburn, 1819).

6. Declaration of Rights—from the Stamp Act Congress

It was owing to England's astronomical debts following the French and Indian War that Parliament began formulating methods to tax the American colonists for their fair share, the most infamous among them being the Stamp Act. The colonists might have been persuaded that it was fair, but no one in Parliament asked. So in June of 1765, delegates from nine colonies accepted the invitation from the Massachusetts Assembly to meet secretly to "consult together on the present circumstances of the colonies," particularly the Stamp Act. This meeting, the Stamp Act Congress, resulted in an October 19th adoption of a "Declaration of Rights and Grievances" that they sent as petitions to the king and Parliament. Despite the relative diplomatic tone of the petitions, however, Parliament refused to receive them.

The members of this Congress, sincerely devoted, with the warmest sentiments of affection and duty to his Majesty's person and government, inviolably attached to the present happy establishment of the Protestant succession, and with minds deeply impressed by a sense of the present and impending misfortunes of the British Colonies on this continent; having considered as maturely as time will permit, the circumstances of the said colonies, esteem it our indispensable duty to make the following declarations of our humble opinion, respecting the most essential rights and liberties of the colonists, and of the grievances under which they labour, by reason of several late Acts of Parliament.

I. That his Majesty's subjects in these colonies owe the same allegiance to the Crown of Great Britain, that is owing from his subjects born within the realm, and all due subordination to that august body, the Parliament of Great Britain.

II. That his Majesty's liege subjects in these colonies are intitled to all the inherent rights and liberties of his natural born subjects, within the kingdom of Great Britain.

III. That it is inseparably essential to the freedom of a people, and the undoubted right of Englishmen, that no Taxes be imposed on them but with their own consent, given personally, or by their representatives.

IV. That the people of these colonies are not, and, from their local circumstances cannot be, represented in the House of Commons in Great Britain.

V. That the only representatives of the people of these colonies are persons chosen therein by themselves, and that no taxes ever have been, or can be constitutionally imposed on them, but by their respective legislatures.

VI. That all supplies to the Crown being free gifts of the people, it is unreasonable and inconsistent with the principles and spirit of the British Constitution, for the people of Great Britain to grant to his Majesty the property of the colonists.

VII. That trial by jury is the inherent and invaluable right of every British subject in these colonies.

VIII. That—[the Stamp Act] . . . by imposing taxes on the inhabitants of these colonies, and the said Act, and several other Acts, by extending the jurisdiction of the courts of admiralty beyond its ancient limits, have a manifest tendency to subvert the rights and liberties of the colonists.

IX. That the duties imposed by several late Acts of Parliament, from the peculiar circumstances of these colonies, will be extremely burthensome and grievous; and from the scarcity of specie, the payment of them absolutely unpracticable.

X. That as the profits of the trade of these colonies ultimately centre in Great Britain, to pay for the manufactures which they are obliged to take from thence, they eventually contribute very largely to all supplies granted there to the Crown.

XI. That the restrictions imposed by several late Acts of Parliament on the trade of these colonies, will render them unable to purchase the manufactures of Great Britain.

XII. That the increase, prosperity, and happiness of these colonies, depend on the full and free enjoyments of their rights and liberties, and an intercourse with Great Britain mutually affectionate and advantageous.

XIII. That it is the right of the British subjects in these colonies to petition the King, or either House of Parliament.

Lastly, That it is the indispensable duty of these colonies, to the best of sovereigns, to the Mother Country, and to themselves, to endeavour by a loyal and dutiful address to his Majesty and humble applications to both Houses of Parliament, to procure the repeal of the Act for granting and applying certain stamp duties, of all clauses of any other Acts of Parliament, Whereby the jurisdiction of the admiralty is extended as aforesaid, and of the other late Acts for the restriction of American Commerce.

Hannis Taylor, *The Origin and Growth of the American Constitution: An Historical Treatise* (Boston: Houghton Mifflin, 1911).

7. Benjamin Franklin's Notions Concerning Trade and Merchants

Americans have always been a people who have valued trade. Then as now, livelihoods depended on it, and people like Benjamin Franklin gave commerce careful consideration. Here he lays out a basic argument for the role of entrepreneurs in an economy, and his insights are as valuable today as when he first penned them.

1. Were it possible for men, remote from each other, to know easily one another's wants and abundances, and practicable for them on all occasions conveniently to meet and make fair exchanges of their respective commodities, there would then be no use of the middle man or merchant; such a profession would not exist.

2. But since that is not possible, were all governments to appoint a number of public officers, whose duty and business it should be to inform themselves thoroughly of those wants and abundances, and to procure, by proper management, all the exchanges that would tend to increase the general happiness, such officers, if they could well discharge their trust, would deserve honors and salaries equivalent to their industry and fidelity.

3. But, as in large communities, and for the more general occasions of mankind, such officers have never been appointed, perhaps from a conviction that it would be *impracticable* for such an appointment effectually to answer its purpose, it seems necessary to permit men, who, for the *possible profits* in prospect, will undertake it, to fetch and

carry, at all distances, the produce of other men's industry, and thereby assist those useful exchanges.

4. As the persons primarily interested in these exchanges cannot conveniently meet to make known their wants and abundances, and to bargain for exchanges, those who transport the goods should be interested to study the probability of these wants, and where to find the means of supplying them; and, since there exist no salaries or public rewards for them in proportion to their skill, industry, and utility to the people in general, nor to make them any compensation for their losses arising from inexpertness or from accident, it seems reasonable that for their encouragement to follow the business, they should be left to make such profits by it as they can, which, where it is open to all, will probably seldom be extravagant. And perhaps by this means the business will be better done for the general advantage, and those who do it more properly rewarded according to their merits, than would be the case were special officers to be appointed for that service.

Benjamin Franklin, *Memoirs of the Life and Writings of Benjamin Franklin*, vol. 6, 3rd ed. (London: Henry Colburn, 1833).

8. JOHN DICKINSON'S "THE LIBERTY SONG"

Dickinson's ditty was famous in its day, sung from one end of the colonies to the other at patriotic gatherings, at taverns, on local commons and public grounds, and at protests and celebrations.

> Come, join hand in hand, brave Americans all,
> And rouse your bold hearts at fair Liberty's call;

No tyrannous act shall suppress your just claim,
Or stain with dishonour America's name.

In freedom we're born, and in freedom we'll live;
    Our purses are ready,
    Steady, Friends, steady,
Not as slaves, but as freemen our money we'll give.

Our worthy forefathers (let's give them a cheer)
To climates unknown did courageously steer;
Through oceans to deserts for freedom they came,
And dying bequeath'd us their freedom and fame.

In freedom we're born, etc.

How sweet are the labours that freemen endure,
That they shall enjoy all the profit, secure—
No more such sweet labors Americans know,
If Britons shall reap what Americans sow.

In freedom we're born, etc.

Swarms of placemen and pensioners soon will appear,
Like locusts deforming the charms of the year;
Suns vainly will rise, showers vainly descend,
If we are to drudge for what others shall spend.

In freedom we're born, etc.

Then join hand in hand, brave Americans all,
By uniting we stand by dividing, we fall;
In so righteous a cause let us hope to succeed,
For Heaven approves of each generous deed.

In freedom we're born, etc. . . .

Percy H. Boynton, ed., *American Poetry* (New York: C. Scribner's Sons, 1918).

SAMUEL ADAMS. Image source: U.S. History Images, from *A Popular History of the United States*, by William Cullen Bryant, and Howard Gay Sydney (New York: Charles Sribners' Sons, 1881).

9. SAMUEL ADAMS ON THE RIGHTS OF THE AMERICANS

John Adams's older cousin was a force to be reckoned with in Boston—a rabble rouser, an activist, a pundit, an organizer, an advocate, and a fearless champion of the rights of Americans in the face of English encroachments. This example is from the December 23, 1771, Boston Gazette, and features arguments typical of Adams and the patriots.

Messieurs EDES & GILL,

The writer in the Massachusetts Gazette, who signs Chronus, in his address to the publick, recommended petitioning and humbly representing the hardship of certain measures; and yet before he finished his first paper, he pointed out to us the unhappy effects in former times of the very method he had prescribed. Those "intemperate patriots" it seems, the majority of both houses of the general assembly, not hearkning to the cool advice of the *few wise men* within and without doors, must needs make their humble representations to the King and Council upon the claims of New-Hampshire and Rhode-Island: And what was the consequence? Why, he says the province lost ten times the value of the land in dispute. Did Chronus mean by this and such like instances, to enforce the measure which he had recommended? They certainly afford a poor encouragement for us to persevere in the way of petitioning and humble representation. But perhaps he will say, the General Assembly had at that time no reason to complain of the incroachment of these sister colonies; their claims were just; and the *discerning few* who were in that mind were in the right. Just so he says is the case now. For he tells us that "no one has attempted to infringe the peoples rights." Upon what principle then would he have us petition? It is possible, for I would fain understand him, that what Candidus and others call an *invasion of our rights*, he may choose to denominate a *Grievance*; for if we suffer no Grievance, he can certainly have no reason to advise us to represent the hardship of certain measures. And I am the rather inclin'd to think, that this is his particular humour, because I find that the stamp-act, which almost every one looked upon as a most *violent infraction* of our natural and constitutional rights, is called by this writer a *Grievance*. And he is so singular as to enquire, "What *Liberties* we are now deprived of," altho' an act of parliament is still in being, and daily executed, very similar to the stamp-act, and form'd for the very *same purpose*, viz. the raising and establishing a revenue in the colonies by virtue of a suppos'd inherent right in the British parliament, where the colonies cannot be represented, and therefore without their consent. The exercise of such a power Chronus would have us consider as a *Grievance* indeed, but not by any means a deprivation of our rights and liberties, or even so much as the least *infringement* of them. Mr. Locke has often been quoted in the present dispute between Britain and her colonies, and very much to our purpose. His reasoning is so forcible, that no one has even attempted to confute it. He holds that "the preservation of property is the end of government, and that for which men enter into society. It therefore necessarily supposes and requires that the people should have property, without which they must be suppos'd to lose that by entering into society, which was the *end* for which they enter'd into it; too gross an absurdity for any man to own. Men therefore *in society having property*, they have such a right to the goods, which by the law of the community are theirs, that no body hath the right to take *any part* of their subsistence from them without their consent: Without this, they could have no property at all. For I truly can have no property in that which another can by right take from me when he pleases, against my consent. Hence, says he, it is a mistake to think that the supreme power of any common-wealth can dispose of the estates of the subjects arbitrarily, or *take any part of them* at pleasure. The prince or senate can never have a power to take to themselves the whole or any part of the subjects property without *their own* consent; for this would be in effect to have *no property* at all."—This is the reasoning of that great and good man. And is not our own case exactly described by him? Hath not the British parliament made an act to take *a part* of our property against our *consent*? Against our repeated submissive petitions and humble representations of the hardship of it? Is not the act daily executed in every colony? If therefore the preservation of property is the very *end* of government, we are depriv'd of that for which government itself is instituted.—Tis true, says Mr. Locke, "Government cannot be supported without great charge; and tis fit that every one who enjoys a share in the pro-tection should pay his proportion for the maintenance of it. But still it must be with their own *consent*, given by themselves or their representatives." Chronus will not say that the monies that are every day paid at the custom-houses in America for the express purpose of maintaining all or any of the Governors therein, were rais'd with the *consent* of those who pay them, given by themselves or their representatives—"If any one, adds Mr. Locke, shall *claim* a power to lay and levy taxes on the people by his own authority & without such *consent* of the people, he thereby *subverts the end of government*."—Will Chronus tell us that the British parliament doth not *claim* authority to lay and levy such taxes, and doth not actually lay and levy them on the colonies without their *consent*? This is the case particularly in this province. If therefore it is a *sub-version of the end of government*, it must be a subversion of our civil liberty, which is supported by civil government only. And this I think a sufficient answer to a strange question which Chronus thinks it "not improper["] for our zealous Patriots to answer, viz. What those liberties and rights are of which we have been deprived.—If Chronus is really as ignorant as he pretends to be, of the present state of the colonies, their universal and just complaints of the most violent infractions of their liberties, and their repeated petitions to the throne upon that account, I hope I shall be excused in taking up any room in your valuable paper, with a view of answering a question, which to him must be of the utmost importance.—But if he is not, I think his question not only impertinent, but a gross affront to the understanding of the public. We have lost the *constitutional right* which the Commons of America in their several Assemblies have ever before possessed, of giving and granting *their own money, as much* of it as they please, and *no more*; and appropriating it for the support of their *own government*, for *their own* defence, and such other purposes as *they please*.—The great Mr. Pitt, in his speech in parliament in favor of the repeal of the stamp-act, declared that "we should have been *slaves* if we had not enjoy'd this right." This is the sentiment of that patriotic member, and it is obvious to the common sense of every man.—If the parliament have a right to take as much of our money as *they please*, they may take *all*. And what liberty can that man have, the produce of whose daily labour *another* has the right to take from him if he pleases, and which is similar to our case, takes *a part* of it to convince him that he has the *power* as well as the pretence of right?—That sage of the law Lord Camden declar'd, in his speech upon the declaratory bill, that "his searches had more and more convinced him that the British parliament have no right to tax the Americans.["] Nor, said he, "is the doctrine new: It is as old as the *constitution*: Indeed, it is its *support*." The taking away this right must then be in the opinion of that great lawyer, the removal of the very *support* of the constitution, upon which all our civil liberties depend. He speaks in still stronger terms—"Taxation and representation are inseparably united: This position is founded on the laws of *nature*: It is more: *It is itself an eternal law of nature*—Whatever is a man's own is absolutely his own; and no man has a right to take it from him without his consent, either express'd by himself or his representative—Whoever attempts to do it, attempts an *injury* : Whoever does it, commits a ROBBERY: *He throws down the distinction between liberty and slavery*"—Can Chronus say, that the Americans ever *consented* either by themselves or their representatives, that the British parliament should tax them? That they have taxed us we all know: We all *feel* it : I wish we felt it *more sensibly* : They have therefore, according to the sentiments of the last mention'd Nobleman, which are built on nature and common reason, thrown down the very distinction between liberty and slavery in America— And yet this writer, like one just awoke from a long dream, or, as I cannot help thinking there are good grounds to suspect, with a design to "mislead his unwary readers["] (and unwary they must needs be, if they are thus misled,) to believe that all our liberties are perfectly secure, he calls upon us to show "which of our liberties we are deprived of;" and in the face of a whole continent, as well as of the best men in Europe, he has the effrontery to assert, without the least shadow of argument, that "no one has attempted to infringe them." One cannot after all this, be at a loss to conceive, what judgment to form of his modesty, his understanding or sincerity.

It might be easy to show that there are other instances in which we are deprived of our liberties.—I should think, a people would hardly be perswaded to believe that they were in the full enjoyment of their liberties, while their capital fortress is garrison'd by troops over which they have no controul, and under the direction of an administration in whom, to say the least, they have no reason to place the smallest confidence that they shall be employ'd for their protection, and not as they have been for their destruction—While they have a governor absolutely independent of them for his support, which support as well as his *political being* depends upon that same administration, tho' at the expence of their own money taken from them against their *consent*—While their governor acts not according to the dictates of his own judgment, assisted by the *constitutional advice* of his council, if he thinks it necessary to call for it, but according to the edicts of *such* an administration—Will it mend the matter that this governor, thus *dependent upon the crown*, is to be the judge of the *legality* of instructions and their consistency with the Charter, which is the constitution? Or if their present governor should be possess'd of as many angelic properties as we have heard of in the late addresses, can they enjoy that tranquility of mind arising from their sense of safety, which

Montesquieu defines to be civil liberty, when they consider how *precarious* a person a provincial governor is, especially a *good one?* And how likely a thing it is, *if he is* a good one, that another may soon be placed in his stead, possessed of the principles of the Devil, who for the sake of holding his commission which is even now pleaded as a weighty motive, will execute to the full the orders of an abandon'd minister, to the ruin of those liberties which we are told are now so secure—Will a people be perswaded that their liberties are safe, while their representatives in general assembly, if they are ever to meet again, will be deprived of the most essential privilege of giving and granting what *part* of their own money they are yet allowed to give and grant, unless, in conformity to a ministerial instruction to the governor, solemnly read to them for their *direction*, they exempt the commissioners of the customs, or any other *favorites or tools* of the ministry, from their *equitable* share in the tax? All these and many others that might be mention'd, are the *natural* effects of that capital cause of complaint of all North-America, which, to use the language of those "intemperate patriots", the majority of the present assembly, is "a subjugation to as arbitrary a TRIBUTE as ever the Romans laid upon the Jews, or their other colonies"—What now is the advice of Chronus? Why, "much may be done, says he, by humble petitions and representations of the *hardship* of certain measures"—Ask him whether the colonies have not already done it? Whether the assembly of this province, the convention, the town of Boston, have not petitioned and humbly represented the hardship of certain measures, and all to no purpose, and he tells you either that he is "a stranger to those petitions", or "that they were not duly timed, or properly urged," or "that the true reason why ALL our petitions and representations met with no better success was, because they were accompanied with a conduct quite the reverse of that submission and duty which they seem'd to express"—that "to present a petition with one hand, while the other is held up in a threatning posture to enforce it, is not the way to succeed"—Search for his meaning, and enquire when the threatning hand was held up, and you'll find him encountering the Resolves of the Town of Boston to maintain their Rights, (in which they copied after the patriotic Assemblies of the several Colonies) and their Instructions to their Representatives. Here is the sad source of all our difficulties.—Chronus would have us petition, and humbly represent the hardships of certain measures, but we must by no means *assert our Liberties.* We must acknowledge, at least *tacitly,* that the Parliament of Great Britain has a constitutional authority, "to throw down the distinction between Liberty and slavery" in America. We may indeed, humbly represent it as a *hardship,* but if they are resolved to execute the purpose, we must submit to it, without the least intimation to posterity, that we look'd upon it as unconstitutional or unjust. Such advice was sagely given to the Colonists a few years ago, at second hand, by one who had taken a trip to the great city, and grew wonderfully acquainted, as he said, with Lord Hillsborough; but his foibles are now "buried under the mantle of charity." Very different was his advice from that of another of infinitely greater abilities, as well as experience in the public affairs of the nation, and the colonies: I mean

Doctor Benjamin Franklin, the present agent of the House of Representatives. His last letter to his constituents, as I am well informed, strongly recommends the holding up our constitutional Rights, by *frequent Resolves, &c.* This we know will be obnoxious to those who are in the plan to enslave us: But remember my countrymen, it will be better to have your liberties wrested from you by *force*, than to have it said that you even implicitly *surrendered* them.

I have something more to say to Chronus when leisure will admit of it.

—CANDIDUS

Harry Cushing, ed., *The Writings of Samuel Adams*, vol. 2 (New York: G.P. Putnam's Sons, 1906).

10. REV. SAMUEL COOKE, AN ELECTION SERMON (1770)

One of Rev. Samuel Cooke's (1709–1783) finest hours was when he gave the annual election day sermon to the Massachusetts General Court. It was May of 1770, not too long after the Boston Massacre, when he delivered this sermon railing against abuse of power by those in authority. His commentary on principles such as the right of the people to choose who will rule them and the importance of checks on power in government reflect the feelings of the times.

HE THAT RULETH OVER MEN MUST BE JUST, RULING IN THE FEAR OF GOD. AND HE SHALL BE AS THE LIGHT

OF THE MORNING WHEN THE SUN RISETH, EVEN A
MORNING WITHOUT CLOUDS: AS THE TENDER GRASS
SPRINGING OUT OF THE EARTH BY CLEAR SHINING
AFTER RAIN.—2 Sam. xxiii. 3, 4.

The solemn introduction to the words now read,
respectable hearers, is manifestly designed to engage your
attention and regard, as given by inspiration from God, and
as containing the last, the dying words of one of the greatest and best of earthly rulers, who, by ruling in the fear of
God, had served his generation according to the divine will.
Transporting reflection! when his flesh and his heart failed,
and his glory was consigned to dust.

From this and many other passages in the sacred oracles,
it is evident that the Supreme Ruler, though he has directed
to no particular mode of civil government, yet allows and
approves of the establishment of it among men.

The ends of civil government, in divine revelation, are
clearly pointed out, the character of rulers described, and
the duty of subjects asserted and explained; and in this
view civil government may be considered as an ordinance
of God, and, when justly exercised, greatly subservient to
the glorious purposes of divine providence and grace: but
the particular form is left to the choice and determination
of mankind. . . .

When the elections of this important day are determined,
what further remains to be undertaken for the securing our
liberties, promoting peace and good order, and, above all,
the advancement of religion, the true fear of God through

the land, will demand the highest attention of the General Assembly. We trust the Fountain of light, who giveth wisdom freely, will not scatter darkness in your paths, and that the day is far distant when there shall be cause justly to complain, The foundations are destroyed—what can the righteous do? Our present distresses, civil fathers, loudly call upon us all, and you in special, to stir up ourselves in the fear of God. Arise!—this matter belongeth unto you; we also will be with you. Be of good courage, and do it.

Whether any other laws are necessary for this purpose, or whether there is a failure in the execution of the laws in being, I presume not to say. But, with all due respect, I may be permitted to affirm that no human authority can enforce the practice of religion with equal success to your example. Your example, fathers, not only in your public administrations, but also in private life, will be the most forcible law—the most effectual means to teach us the fear of the Lord, and to depart from evil. Then, and not till then, shall we be free indeed; being delivered from the dominion of sin, we become the true sons of God.

The extent of the secular power in matters of religion is undetermined; but all agree that the example of those in authority has the greatest influence upon the manners of the people. We are far from pleading for any established mode of worship, but an operative fear of God, the honor of the Redeemer, the everlasting King, according to his gospel. We, whose peculiar charge it is to instruct the people, preach to little purpose while those in an advanced state, by their practice, say the fear of God is not before their eyes; yet will we not cease to seek the Lord till he come and rain down righteousness upon us.

I trust on this occasion I may without offence plead the cause of our African slaves, and humbly propose the pursuit of some effectual measures at least to prevent the future importation of them. Difficulties insuperable, I apprehend, prevent an adequate remedy for what is past. Let the time past more than suffice wherein we, the patrons of liberty, have dishonored the Christian name, and degraded human nature nearly to a level with the beasts that perish. Ethiopia has long stretched out her hands to us. Let not sordid gain, acquired by the merchandise of slaves and the souls of men, harden our hearts against her piteous moans. When God ariseth, and when he visiteth, what shall we answer? May it be the glory of this province, of this respectable General Assembly, and, we could wish, of this session, to lead in the cause of the oppressed. This will avert the impending vengeance of Heaven, procure you the blessing of multitudes of your fellow-men ready to perish, be highly approved by our common Father, who is no respecter of persons, and, we trust, an example which would excite the highest attention of our sister colonies. May we all, both rulers and people, in this day of doubtful expectation, know and practise the things of our peace, and serve the Lord our God without disquiet in the inheritance which he granted unto our fathers. These adventurous worthies, animated by sublimer prospects, dearly purchased this land with their treasure; they and their posterity have defended it with unknown cost, in continual jeopardy of their lives, and with their blood.

Through the good hands of our God upon us, we have for a few years past been delivered from the merciless sword of the wilderness, and enjoyed peace in our borders; and there is in the close of our short summer the appearance of plenty in our dwellings; but, from the length of our winters, our plenty is consumed, and the one half of our necessary labor is spent in dispersing to our flocks and herds the ingatherings of the foregoing season; and it is known to every person of common observation that few, very few, except in the mercantile way, from one generation to another, acquire more than a necessary subsistence, and sufficient to discharge the expenses of government and the support of the gospel, yet content and disposed to lead peaceable lives. From misinformations only, we would conclude, recent disquiets have arisen. They need not be mentioned—they are too well known; their voice is gone out through all the earth, and their sound to the end of the world. The enemies of Great Britain hold us in derision while her cities and colonies are thus perplexed. America now pleads her right to her possessions, which she cannot resign while she apprehends she has truth and justice on her side.

Americans esteem it their greatest infelicity that, through necessity, they are thus led to plead with their parent state,— the land of their forefathers' nativity,—whose interest has always been dear to them, and whose wealth they have increased by their removal more than their own. They have assisted in fighting her battles, and greatly enlarged her empire, and, God helping, will yet extend it through the boundless desert, until it reach from sea to sea. They glory in the British constitution, and are abhorrent, to a man, of the most distant thought of withdrawing their allegiance from their gracious sovereign and becoming an independent state. And though, with unwearied toil, the colonists can now sub-sist upon the labors of their own hands, which they must be driven to when deprived of the means of purchase, yet they are fully sensible of the mutual benefits of an equitable commerce with the parent country, and cheerfully submit to regulations of trade productive of the common interest. These their claims the Americans consider not as novel, or wantonly made, but founded in nature, in compact, in their right as men and British subjects; the same which their fore-fathers, the first occupants, made and asserted as the terms of their removal, with their effects, into this wilderness, and with which the glory and interest of their king and all his dominions are connected. May these alarming disputes be brought to a just and speedy issue, and peace and harmony be restored!

But while, in imitation of our pious forefathers, we are aiming at the security of our liberties, we should all be concerned to express by our conduct their piety and virtue, and in a day of darkness and general distress carefully avoid everything offensive to God or injurious to men. It belongs not only to rulers, but subjects also, to set the Lord always before their face, and act in his fear. While under government we claim a right to be treated as men, we must act in char-acter by yielding that subjection which becometh us as men. Let every attempt to secure our liberties be conducted with a manly fortitude, but with that respectful decency which reason approves, and which alone gives weight to the most salutary measures. Let nothing divert us from the paths of truth and peace, which are the ways of God, and then we may be sure that he will be with us, as he was with our fathers, and never leave nor forsake us.

Our fathers—where are they? They looked for another and better country, that is, an heavenly. They were but as sojourners here, and have long since resigned these their transitory abodes, and are securely seated in mansions of glory. They hear not the voice of the oppressor. We also are all strangers on earth, and must soon, without distinction, lie down in the dust, and rise not till these heavens and earth are no more. May we all realize the appearance of the Son of God to judge the world in righteousness, and improve the various talents committed to our trust, that we may then lift up our heads with joy, and, through grace, receive an inheritance which cannot be taken away, even life everlasting! AMEN.

John Wingate Thornton, ed., *The Pulpit of the American Revolution* (Boston: Gould and Lincoln, 1860).

11. PAUL REVERE ON THE CAUSE OF THE QUARREL

Thomas Jefferson and Samuel Adams could plumb the philosophical depths of the quarrel between Britain and America and rationalize why the Americans were in the right, but the layman—with no better representative here than the silversmith

*and express rider Paul Revere—knew his way around the con-
flict as well. Instead of references to Lord Coke and John Locke,
the references are to the book of Joshua and Aesop, but the take-
away was the same, as this 1 July 1782 letter to Revere's British
cousin John Rivoire shows.*

You say "we have entered into a war with Brittain against all
laws human & divine." You do not use all the candour which
I am sure you are master of, else you have not looked into
the merits of the quarrel. They covenanted with the first
settlers of this country, that we should enjoy "all the Libertys
of free natural born subjects of Great Britain." They were
not contented to have all the benefit of our trade, in short
to have all our earnings, but they wanted to make us hewers of wood, & drawers of water.* Their Parliament have
declared "that they have a right to tax us & Legislate for
us, in all cases whatsoever"—now certainly if they have a
right to take one shilling from us without our consent, they
have a right to all we possess; for it is the birthright of an
Englishman, not to be taxed without the consent of himself,
or Representative. . . .

You say "You will suppose for one moment that there
is faults on both sides; that is, England & America are both
in fault." The supposition is intirely groundless, the fault is

---

*Editor's Note: An allusion to Joshua 9.27: "And Joshua made them that day
hewers of wood and drawers of water for the congregation, and for the altar
of the LORD. . . ." Since Revere's time, the hewers and drawers reference has
meant someone forced or enslaved to do menial tasks for the benefit of
another.

wholly on the side of England, America took every method in her power by petitioning &c. to remain subject to Brittain; but Brittain (I mean the British King & Ministers) did not want Colonies of *free men* they wanted Colonies of *Slaves.* Like the fable of the Woman & Hen, by grasping at too much they will lose all.*

*Editor's Note: One of Aesop's fables. The woman tries to get two eggs from her hen instead of one and ends up with none.

Elbridge Henry Goss, *The Life of Colonel Paul Revere*, vol. 2 (Boston: Howard W. Spurr, 1898).

12. A Song about the Boston Tea Party

A little ditty about taxes, tea, and tyranny from the year 1773.

> *As near beauteous Boston lying,*
> *On the gently swelling flood,*
> *Without jack or pendant flying,*
> *Three ill-fated tea-ships rode,*
>
> *Just as glorious Sol was setting,*
> *On the wharf a numerous crew,*
> *Sons of freedom, fear forgetting,*
> *Suddenly appeared in view.*
>
> *Armed with hammers, axe, and chisels,*
> *Weapons new for warlike deed,*

Towards the herbage-freighted vessels
They approached with dreadful speed.

O'er their heads aloft in mid-sky
Three bright angel forms were seen:
This was Hampden, that was Sidney,
With fair Liberty between.

"Soon," they cried, "your foes you'll banish,
Soon the triumph shall be won;
Scarce shall setting Phoebus vanish
Ere the deathless deed be done."

Quick as thought the ships were boarded,
Hatches burst and chests displayed;
Axes, hammers help afforded;
What a glorious crash they made!

Squash into the deep descended
Cursed weed of China's coast:
Thus at once our fears were ended—
British rights shall ne'er be lost.

Captains, once more hoist your streamers,
Spread your sails and plough the wave:
Tell your masters they were dreamers,
When they thought to cheat the brave.

Walter C. Bronson, ed., *American Poems (1625–1892)* (Chicago: University of Chicago Press, 1912).

13. George Washington on the Question of Rebellion

From a July 4, 1774, letter to Bryan Fairfax contemplating revolution and the proper response to the ongoing abuses of the imperial government.

John has just delivered to me your favor of yesterday, which I shall be obliged to answer in a more concise manner, than I could wish, as I am very much engaged in raising one of the additions to my house, which I think (perhaps it is fancy) goes on better whilst I am present, than in my absence from the workmen. . . .

As to your political sentiments, I would heartily join you in them, so far as relates to a humble and dutiful petition to the throne, provided there was the most distant hope of success. But have we not tried this already? Have we not addressed the Lords, and remonstrated to the Commons? And to what end? Did they deign to look at our petitions? Does it not appear, as clear as the sun in its meridian brightness, that there is a regular, systematic plan formed to fix the right and practice of taxation upon us? Does not the uniform conduct of Parliament for some years past confirm this? Do not all the debates, especially those just brought to us, in the House of Commons on the side of government, expressly declare that America must be taxed in aid of the British funds, and that she has no longer resources within herself? Is there any thing to be expected from petitioning after this? Is not the attack upon the liberty and property of the people of

Boston, before restitution of the loss to the India Company was demanded, a plain and self-evident proof of what they are aiming at. Do not the subsequent bills (now I dare say acts), for depriving the Massachusetts Bay of its charter, and for transporting offenders into other colonies or to Great Britain for trial, where it is impossible from the nature of the thing that justice can be obtained, convince us that the administration is determined to stick at nothing to carry its point. Ought we not, then, to put our virtue and fortitude to the severest test?

With you I think it a folly to attempt more than we can execute, as that will not only bring disgrace upon us, but weaken our cause; yet I think we may do more than is generally believed, in respect to the non-importation scheme. As to the withholding of our remittances, that is another point, in which I own I have my doubts on several accounts, but principally on that of justice; for I think, whilst we are accusing others of injustice, we should be just ourselves; and how this can be, whilst we owe a considerable debt, and refuse payment of it to Great Britain, is to me inconceivable. Nothing but the last extremity, I think, can justify it. Whether this is now come, is the question. . . .

Jared Sparks, ed., *The Writings of George Washington*, vol. 2 (Boston: Little, Brown, 1855).

III. Revolution

W hat had been building since before Edward Randolph's 1676 report about colonists disregarding England's trade laws and Peter Kalm's 1748 observation about the independence of the colonies and the prospect for separation finally all came to a head.

The tax fights of the 1760s and the unwanted presence of the British troops in the 1770s resulted in an unavoidable escalation that produced open war.

The Americans were hardly ready for Revolution and struggled throughout the effort, being minimally equipped and provisioned. But through the leadership of George Washington and the patient endurance of the populace, along with bravery and sacrifice untold, the colonies finally became independent and free states.

1. A Letter from George Washington to His Generals

April of 1775 set off the American Revolution at Lexington and Concord, June brought the Battle of Bunker Hill, and in July, George Washington assumed command of the main American army at Cambridge, Massachusetts, where it had been laying siege to British-occupied Boston. During the fall Washington wrote many letters, including this one attempting to assure his army would have the necessities to make it through the upcoming winter.

Camp at Cambridge, 8 September, 1775.
Gentlemen,

As I mean to call upon you in a day or two for your opinions upon a point of very great importance to the welfare of this continent in general, and this colony in particular, I think it proper, indeed, an incumbent duty on me, previous to this meeting to intimate to you the end and design of it, that you may have time to consider the matter with that deliberation and attention, which the importance of it requires.

It is to know, whether, in your judgment, we cannot make a successful attack upon the troops at Boston by means of boats, cooperated by an attempt upon their lines at Roxbury. The success of such an enterprise depends, I well know, upon the All-wise Disposer of events, and it is not within the reach of human wisdom to foretell the issue; but if the prospect is fair, the undertaking is justifiable under the following, among other reasons, which might be assigned.

The season is now fast approaching, when warm and comfortable barracks must be erected for the security of the troops against the inclemency of winter. Large and costly provision must be made in the article of wood for the supply of the army; and after all that can be done in this way, it is but too probable that fences, woods, orchards, and even houses themselves will fall a sacrifice to the want of fuel before the end of winter. A very considerable difficulty, if not expense, must accrue on account of clothing for the men now engaged in the service; and if they do not enlist again, this difficulty will be increased to an almost insurmountable degree. Blankets, I am informed, are now much wanted, and not to be got. How then shall we be able to keep soldiers to their duty, already impatient to get home, when they come to feel the severity of winter without proper covering? If this army should not incline to engage for a longer time than the 1st of January, what consequences more certainly can follow, than that you must either be obliged to levy new troops and thereby have two sets, or partly so, in pay at the same time, or by disbanding one before you get the other, expose the country to desolation and the cause perhaps to irretrievable ruin. These things are not unknown to the enemy; perhaps it is the very ground they are building on, if they are not waiting for a large reinforcement; and if they are waiting for succorers, ought it not to give a spur to the attempt? Our powder, not much of which will be consumed in such an enterprise, without any certainty of a supply, is daily wasting; and, to sum up the whole, in spite of every saving that can be made, the expense of supporting this army will so far exceed any idea, that was formed in Congress of it, that I do not know what will be the consequences.

These, among many other reasons, which might be assigned, induce me to wish a speedy finish of the dispute; but to avoid these evils we are not to lose sight of the difficulties, the hazard, and the loss, that may accompany the attempt, nor what will be the probable consequences of a failure.

That every circumstance for and against this measure may be duly weighed, that there may be time for doing it, and nothing of this importance resolved on, but after mature deliberation, I give this previous notice of the intention of calling you together on Monday next at nine o'clock, at which time you are requested to attend at head-quarters. It is not necessary, I am persuaded, to recommend secrecy. The success of the enterprise, (if undertaken,) must depend in a great measure upon the suddenness of the stroke. I am with great esteem, etc.

Worthington Chauncey Ford, ed., *The Writings of George Washington*, vol. 3 (New York: G.P. Putnam's Sons, 1889).

GEORGE WASHINGTON TAKING THE SALUTE AT TRENTON.
Image Source: U.S. Library of Congress. Artist, John Faed.

2. John Dickinson and Thomas Jefferson on the Causes and Necessity of Taking Up Arms, July 6, 1775

In April of 1775, the "shot heard round the world" was fired in Lexington, Massachusetts, thereby beginning the American Revolution. On June 14, 1775, the Second Continental Congress met to adopt the New England army as its own. It also began assembling this Declaration, largely the writing of Thomas Jefferson and John Dickinson, to substantiate the fighting yet to come.

We are reduced to the alternative of choosing an unconditional submission to the tyranny of irritated ministers, or resistance by force.—The latter is our choice.—We have counted the cost of this contest, and find nothing so dreadful as voluntary slavery.—Honor, justice, and humanity, forbid us tamely to surrender that freedom which we received from our gallant ancestors, and which our innocent posterity have a right to receive from us. We cannot endure the infamy and guilt of resigning succeeding generations to that wretchedness which inevitably awaits them, if we basely entail hereditary bondage upon them.

Our cause is just. *Our Union is perfect.* Our internal resources are great, and if necessary, foreign assistance is undoubtedly attainable.—We gratefully acknowledge as signal instances of the Divine favor towards us, that his Providence would not permit us to be called into this severe controversy, until we were grown up to our present strength, had been previously exercised in warlike operations, and possessed of the means of defending ourselves. With hearts fortified with these animating reflections, we most solemnly, before God and the world, *declare*, that, exerting the utmost energy of those powers, which our beneficent Creator hath graciously bestowed upon us, the arms we have been compelled by our enemies to assume, we will, in defiance of every hazard, with unabating firmness and perseverance, employ for the preservation of our liberties; *being with one mind resolved to die freemen rather than to live slaves.*

Lest this declaration should disquiet the minds of our friends and fellow subjects in any part of the empire, we assure them that we mean not to dissolve that union which has so long and so happily subsisted between us, and which we sincerely wish to see restored.—Necessity has not yet driven us into that desperate measure, or induced us to excite any other nation to war against them. We have not raised armies with ambitious designs of separating from Great Britain, and establishing independent States. We fight not for glory or for conquest. We exhibit to mankind the remarkable spectacle of a people attacked by unprovoked armies, without any imputation, or even suspicion of offence. They boast of their privileges and civilization, and yet proffer no milder conditions than servitude or death.

In our own native land, in defence of the freedom that is our birthright, and which we ever enjoyed till the late violation of it—for the protection of our property, acquired solely by the honest industry of our forefathers and ourselves, against violence actually offered, we have taken up arms. We shall lay them down when hostilities shall cease on the part of the aggressors, and all danger of their being renewed shall be removed, and not before.

With an humble confidence in the mercies of the supreme and impartial Judge and Ruler of the Universe, we most devoutly implore his Divine goodness to protect us happily through this great conflict, to dispose our adversaries to reconciliation on reasonable terms, and thereby to relieve the empire from the calamities of civil war.

Thaddeus Allen, *An Inquiry into the Views, Services, Principles and Influences of the Leading Men in the Origination of Our Union and the Formation and Administration of our Early Government*, vol. 1 (Boston: Saxton & Kelt, 1847).

3. George Washington Fixes a Date to Cross the Delaware

After the fall of Fort Washington, the colonial army had fallen back toward Philadelphia and held their line on the Delaware River. In December of 1776, Colonel Joseph Reed had begged Washington for action by the army in New Jersey, and the plan was conceived to cross the Delaware River and initiate action against the enemy at Trenton. It was to be a major turning point in the war: victories in the Jersey campaign at Trenton and Princeton turned the tide.

TO JOSEPH REED, ESQ.
OR IN HIS ABSENCE TO JOHN CADWALADER, ESQ.,
ONLY, AT BRISTOL.
      —Camp above Trenton Falls, 23d December, 1776.

DEAR SIR,

The bearer is sent down to know whether your plan was attempted last night, and if not to inform you that Christmas day at night, one hour before day is the time fixed upon for our attempt on Trenton. For Heaven's sake, keep this to yourself, as the discovery of it may prove fatal to us; our numbers, sorry am I to say, being less than I had any conception of; but necessity, dire necessity will, nay must, justify my attack. Prepare, and in concert with Griffin, attack as many of their posts as you possibly can, with a prospect of success; the more we can attack at the same instant, the more confusion we shall spread and greater good will result from it. If I had not been fully convinced before of the enemy's designs, I have now ample testimony of their intentions to attack Philadelphia so soon as the ice will afford the means of conveyance. As the colonels of the Continental regiments might kick up some dust about command unless Cadwallader is considered by them in the light of a Brigadier, which I wish him to be, I desired General Gates, who is unwell and applied for leave to go to Philadelphia, to endeavour if his health would permit him, to call and stay two or three days at Bristol in his way. I shall not be particular; we could not ripen matters for our attack before the time mentioned in the first part of this letter, so much out of sorts, and so much in want of every thing are the troops under Sullivan, &c. Let me know by a careful express the plan you are to pursue. The letter herewith sent, forward on to Philadelphia. I could wish it to be in in time for the Southern post's departure, which will be, I believe by eleven o'clock to-morrow. I am, dear sir,

—Your most obedient servant,
George Washington.

William Bradford Reed, ed., *Life and Correspondence of Joseph Reed: Military Secretary of Washington at Cambridge*, vol. I (Philadelphia: Lindsay and Blakiston, 1847).

4. "The Battle of Trenton" (1776)

The British Army grew overconfident and careless, and Howe and Cornwallis returned to New York for Christmas. In a surprise attack, Washington and his troops crossed the icy Delaware River to attack at daybreak. The Americans lost only four men, but the enemy was routed: eighteen were killed and over a thousand made prisoners. The remainder retreated, leaving everything—including their sick and wounded—behind.

> *On Christmas-day in seventy-six,*
> *Our ragged troops, with bayonets fixed,*
>   *For Trenton marched away.*
> *The Delaware see! the boats below!*
> *The light obscured by hail and snow!*
>   *But no signs of dismay.*
>
> *Our object was the Hessian band,*
> *That dared invade fair freedom's land,*
>   *And quarter in that place.*
> *Great Washington he led us on,*
> *Whose streaming flag, in storm or sun,*
>   *Had never known disgrace.*

In silent march we passed the night,
Each soldier panting for the fight,
    Though quite benumbed with frost.
Greene on the left at six began,
The right was led by Sullivan
    Who ne'er a moment lost.

Their pickets stormed, the alarm was spread,
That rebels risen from the dead
    Were marching into town.
Some scampered here, some scampered there,
And some for action did prepare;
    But soon their arms laid down.

Twelve hundred servile miscreants,
With all their colors, guns, and tents,
    Were trophies of the day.
The frolic o'er, the bright canteen,
In centre, front, and rear was seen
    Driving fatigue away.

Now, brothers of the patriot bands,
Let's sing deliverance from the hands
    Of arbitrary sway.
And as our life is but a span,
Let's touch the tankard while we can,
    In memory of that day.

Burton Egbert Stevenson, ed., *Poems of American History* (Boston: Houghton Mifflin, 1922).

5. Richard Henry Lee Offers "Certain Resolutions," in the Congress (June 7, 1776)

On June 7, 1776, a remarkable assembly of men gathered in the Pennsylvania State House in Philadelphia, representing thousands who were ready to die freemen rather than live as slaves. Richard Henry Lee, a Representative from Virginia, arose and offered "Certain resolutions."

Resolved, That these United Colonies are, and of right ought to be, free and independent States; that they are absolved from all allegiance to the British Crown, and that all political connection between them and the State of Great Britain is, and ought to be, totally dissolved.

That it is expedient forthwith to take the most effectual measures for forming foreign alliances.

That a plan of confederation be prepared and transmitted to the respective Colonies for their consideration and approbation.

Worthington Chauncey Ford, ed., *Journals of the Continental Congress, 1774–1789*, vol. 5 (Washington: Government Printing Office, 1906).

6. John Adams's Letter to William Cushing (June 9, 1776)

During the momentous days leading up to the Declaration of Independence, John Adams wrote a letter to his friend about "a revolution, the most remarkable, of any."

It would give me great pleasure to ride this eastern circuit with you, and prate before you at the bar, as I used to do. But I am destined to another fate, to drudgery of the most wasting, exhausting, consuming kind, that I ever went through in my whole life. Objects of the most stupendous magnitude, and measures in which the lives and liberties of millions yet unborn are intimately interested, are now before us. We are in the very midst of a revolution, the most complete, unexpected, and remarkable, of any in the history of nations. A few important subjects must be despatched before I can return to my family. Every colony must be induced to institute a perfect government. All the colonies must confederate together in some solemn band of union. The Congress must declare the colonies free and independent States, and ambassadors must be sent abroad to foreign courts, to solicit their acknowledgment of us, as sovereign States, and to form with them, at least with some of them, commercial treaties of friendship and alliance. When these things are once completed, I shall think that I have answered the end of my creation, and sing my *nunc dimittis*, return to my farm, family, ride circuits, plead law, or judge causes, just which you please.

Charles Francis Adams, ed., *The Works of John Adams*, vol. 9 (Boston: Little, Brown, 1854).

7. THE TIMES THAT TRY MEN'S SOULS

From The American Crisis, *by Thomas Paine, 1776.*

These are the times that try men's souls. The summer soldier and the sunshine patriot will, in this crisis, shrink from the service of their country; but he that stands it *now*, deserves the love and thanks of man and woman. Tyranny, like hell, is not easily conquered; yet we have this consolation with us, that the harder the conflict, the more glorious the triumph. What we obtain too cheap, we esteem too lightly: it is dearness only that gives every thing its value. Heaven knows how to put a proper price upon its goods; and it would be strange indeed if so celestial an article as Freedom should not be highly rated. Britain, with an army to enforce her tyranny, has declared that she has a right (*not only to* Tax) but "to Bind us in All Cases Whatsoever," and if being *bound in that manner*, is not slavery, then there is not such a thing as slavery upon earth. Even the expression is impious; for so unlimited a power can belong only to God.

Whether the independence of the continent was declared too soon, or delayed too long, I will not now enter into as an argument; my own simple opinion is, that had it been eight months earlier, it would have been much better. We did not make a proper use of last winter, neither could we, while we were in a dependent state. However, the fault, if it were one, was all our own;* we have none to blame but ourselves. But no great deal is lost yet. All that Howe has been doing for this month past, is rather a ravage than a conquest, which the spirit of the Jerseys, a year ago, would have quickly repulsed, and which time and a little resolution will soon recover.

---

* *The present winter is worth an age, if rightly employed; but, if lost or neglected, the whole continent will partake of the evil; and there is no punishment that man does not deserve, be he who, or what, or where he will, that may be the means of sacrificing a season so precious and useful.*

I have as little superstition in me as any man living, but my secret opinion has ever been, and still is, that God Almighty will not give up a people to military destruction, or leave them unsupportedly to perish, who have so earnestly and so repeatedly sought to avoid the calamities of war, by every decent method which wisdom could invent. Neither have I so much of the infidel in me, as to suppose that He has relinquished the government of the world, and given us up to the care of devils; and as I do not, I cannot see on what grounds the king of Britain can look up to heaven for help against us: a common murderer, a highwayman, or a house-breaker, has as good a pretence as he. . . .

As I was with the troops at Fort Lee, and marched with them to the edge of Pennsylvania, I am well acquainted with many circumstances, which those who live at a distance know but little or nothing of. Our situation there was exceedingly cramped, the place being a narrow neck of land between the North River and the Hackensack. Our force was inconsiderable, being not one fourth so great as Howe could bring against us. We had no army at hand to have relieved the garrison, had we shut ourselves up and stood on our defence. Our ammunition, light artillery, and the best part of our stores, had been removed, on the apprehension that Howe would endeavor to penetrate the Jerseys, in which case Fort Lee could be of no use to us; for it must occur to every thinking man, whether in the army or not, that these kind of field forts are only for temporary purposes, and last in use no longer than the enemy directs his force against the particular object, which such forts are raised to defend. Such was our situation and condition at fort Lee on the morning of the 20th of November, when an officer arrived with information that the enemy with 200 boats had landed about seven miles above: Major General Green, who commanded the garrison, immediately ordered them under arms, and sent express to General Washington at the town of Hackensack, distant by the way of the ferry = six miles. Our first object was to secure the bridge over the Hackensack, which laid up the river between the enemy and us, about six miles from us, and three from them. General Washington arrived in about three quarters of an hour, and marched at the head of the troops towards the bridge, which place I expected we should have a brush for; however, they did not choose to dispute it with us, and the greatest part of our troops went over the bridge, the rest over the ferry, except some which passed at a mill on a small creek, between the bridge and the ferry, and made their way through some marshy grounds up to the town of Hackensack, and there passed the river. We brought off as much baggage as the wagons could contain, the rest was lost. The simple object was to bring off the garrison, and march them on till they could be strengthened by the Jersey or Pennsylvania militia, so as to be enabled to make a stand. We staid four days at Newark, collected our out-posts with some of the Jersey militia, and marched out twice to meet the enemy, on being informed that they were advancing, though our numbers were greatly inferior to theirs. Howe, in my little opinion, committed a great error in generalship in not throwing a body of forces off from Staten Island through Amboy, by which means he might have seized all our stores at Brunswick, and intercepted our march into Pennsylvania; but if we believe the power of hell to be limited, we must likewise believe that their agents are under some providential controul.

I shall not now attempt to give all the particulars of our retreat to the Delaware; suffice it for the present to say, that both officers and men, though greatly harrassed and fatigued, frequently without rest, covering, or provision, the inevitable consequences of a long retreat, bore it with a manly and martial spirit. All their wishes centered in one, which was, that the country would turn out and help them to drive the enemy back. Voltaire has remarked that King William never appeared to full advantage but in difficulties and in action; the same remark may be made on General Washington, for the character fits him. There is a natural firmness in some minds which cannot be unlocked by trifles, but which, when unlocked, discovers a cabinet of fortitude; and I reckon it among those kind of public blessings, which we do not immediately see, that God hath blessed him with uninterrupted health, and given him a mind that can even flourish upon care.

I shall conclude this paper with some miscellaneous remarks on the state of our affairs; and shall begin with asking the following question, Why is it that the enemy have left the New-England provinces, and made these middle ones the seat of war? The answer is easy: New-England is not infested with tories, and we are. I have been tender in raising the cry against these men, and used numberless arguments to show them their danger, but it will not do to sacrifice a world either to their folly or their baseness. The period is now arrived, in which either they or we must change our sentiments, or one or both must fall. And what is a tory? Good God! what is he? I should not be afraid to go with a hundred whigs against a thousand tories, were they to attempt to get into arms. Every tory is a coward; for servile, slavish, self-interested fear is the foundation of toryism; and a man under such influence, though he may be cruel, never can be brave.

But, before the line of irrecoverable separation be drawn between us, let us reason the matter together: Your conduct is an invitation to the enemy, yet not one in a thousand of you has heart enough to join him. Howe is as much deceived by you as the American cause is injured by you. He expects you will all take up arms, and flock to his standard, with muskets on your shoulders. Your opinions are of no use to him, unless you support him personally, for 'tis soldiers, and not tories, that he wants.

I once felt all that kind of anger, which a man ought to feel, against the mean principles that are held by the tories: a noted one, who kept a tavern at Amboy, was standing at his door, with as pretty a child in his hand, about eight or nine years old, as ever I saw, and after speaking his mind as freely as he thought was prudent, finished with this unfatherly expression, "*Well! give me peace in my day.*" Not a man lives on the continent but fully believes that a separation must some time or other finally take place, and a generous parent should have said, "*If there must be trouble, let it be in my day, that my child may have peace;*" and this single reflection, well applied, is sufficient to awaken every man to duty. Not a place upon earth might be so happy as America. Her situation is remote from all the wrangling world, and she has nothing to do but to trade with them. A man can distinguish himself between temper and principle, and I am as confident, as I am that God governs the world, that America will never be happy till she gets clear of foreign dominion. Wars, without ceasing, will break out till that period arrives, and the continent must in the end be conqueror; for though the flame of liberty may sometimes cease to shine, the coal can never expire . . .

William B. Cairns, ed., *Selections from Early American Writers*, 1607–1800 (New York: Macmillan, 1909).

DRAFTING THE DECLARATION OF INDEPENDENCE. Image Source: U.S. History Images, from *American's Story for America's Children: The Early Colonies*, by Mara L. Pratt (Boston: D.C. Heath & Company, 1901).

8. THE DECLARATION OF INDEPENDENCE, JULY 4, 1776

The Declaration is the philosophical defense of the separation from England as well as a list of grievances that form the rationale for having our own go at things. Many founders wrote about the importance of government in securing happiness for its people; it's important to realize that these references are about the private citizen's right to pursue happiness, not the role of the state in providing for the happiness of its people—especially at the expense of other citizens.

When in the Course of human events, it becomes necessary for one people to dissolve the political bands which have connected them with another, and to assume among the powers of the earth, the separate and equal station to which the Laws of Nature and of Nature's God entitle them, a decent respect to the opinions of mankind requires that they should declare the causes which impel them to the separation.

We hold these truths to be self-evident, that all men are created equal, that they are endowed by their Creator with certain unalienable Rights, that among these are Life, Liberty, and the pursuit of Happiness.—That to secure these rights, Governments are instituted among Men, deriving their just powers from the consent of the governed,—that whenever any Form of Government becomes destructive of these ends, it is the Right of the People to alter or to abolish it, and to institute new Government, laying its foundation on such principles and organizing its powers in such form, as to them shall seem most likely to effect their Safety and Happiness. Prudence, indeed, will dictate that Governments long established should not be changed for light and transient causes; and accordingly all experience hath shewn, that mankind are more disposed to suffer, while evils are sufferable, than to right themselves by abolishing the forms to which they are accustomed. But when a long train of abuses and usurpations, pursuing invariably the same Object evinces a design to reduce them under absolute Despotism, it is their right, it is their duty, to throw off such Government, and to provide new Guards for their future security.—Such has been the patient sufferance of these Colonies; and such is now the necessity which constrains them to alter their former Systems of Government. The history of the present King of Great Britain is a history of repeated injuries and usurpations, all having in direct object the establishment of an absolute Tyranny over these States. To prove this, let Facts be submitted to a candid world.

He has refused his Assent to Laws, the most wholesome and necessary for the public good.

He has forbidden his Governors to pass Laws of immediate and pressing importance, unless suspended in their operation till his Assent should be obtained; and when so suspended, he has utterly neglected to attend to them.

He has refused to pass other Laws for the accommodation of large districts of people, unless those people would relinquish the right of Representation in the Legislature, a right inestimable to them, and formidable to tyrants only.

He has called together legislative bodies at places unusual, uncomfortable, and distant from the depository of their public Records, for the sole purpose of fatiguing them into compliance with his measures.

He has dissolved Representative Houses repeatedly, for opposing with manly firmness his invasions on the rights of the people.

He has refused for a long time, after such dissolutions, to cause others to be elected; whereby the Legislative powers, incapable of Annihilation, have returned to the People at large for their exercise; the State remaining in the mean time exposed to all the dangers of invasion from without, and convulsions within.

He has endeavored to prevent the population of these States; for that purpose obstructing the Laws for Naturalization of Foreigners; refusing to pass others to encourage their migrations hither, and raising the conditions of new Appropriations of Lands.

He has obstructed the Administration of Justice, by refusing his Assent to Laws for establishing Judiciary powers.

He has made Judges dependent on his Will alone, for the tenure of their offices, and the amount and payment of their salaries.

He has erected a multitude of New Offices, and sent hither swarms of Officers to harass our people, and eat out their substance.

He has kept among us, in times of peace, Standing Armies without the Consent of our legislatures.

He has affected to render the Military independent of and superior to the Civil power.

He has combined with others to subject us to a jurisdiction foreign to our constitution, and unacknowledged by our laws; giving his Assent to their Acts of pretended Legislation:

For Quartering large bodies of armed troops among us:

For protecting them, by a mock Trial, from punishment for any Murders which they should commit on the Inhabitants of these States:

For cutting off our Trade with all parts of the world:

For imposing Taxes on us without our Consent:

For depriving us in many cases, of the benefits of Trial by Jury:

For transporting us beyond Seas to be tried for pretended offenses

For abolishing the free System of English Laws in a neighbouring Province, establishing therein an Arbitrary government, and enlarging its Boundaries so as to render it at once an example and fit instrument for introducing the same absolute rule into these Colonies:

For taking away our Charters, abolishing our most valuable Laws, and altering fundamentally the Forms of our Governments:

For suspending our own Legislatures, and declaring themselves invested with power to legislate for us in all cases whatsoever.

He has abdicated Government here, by declaring us out of his Protection and waging War against us.

He has plundered our seas, ravaged our Coasts, burnt our towns, and destroyed the lives of our people.

He is at this time transporting large Armies of foreign Mercenaries to complete the works of death, desolation and tyranny, already begun with circumstances of Cruelty & perfidy scarcely paralleled in the most barbarous ages, and totally unworthy the Head of a civilized nation.

He has constrained our fellow Citizens taken Captive on the high Seas to bear Arms against their Country, to become the executioners of their friends and Brethren, or to fall themselves by their Hands.

He has excited domestic insurrections amongst us, and has endeavored to bring on the inhabitants of our frontiers, the merciless Indian Savages, whose known rule of warfare, is an undistinguished destruction of all ages, sexes and conditions.

In every stage of these Oppressions We have Petitioned for Redress in the most humble terms: Our repeated Petitions have been answered only by repeated injury. A Prince whose character is thus marked by every act which may define a Tyrant, is unfit to be the ruler of a free people.

Nor have We been wanting in our attentions to our

British brethren. We have warned them from time to time of attempts by their legislature to extend an unwarrantable jurisdiction over us. We have reminded them of the circumstances of our emigration and settlement here. We have appealed to their native justice and magnanimity, and we have conjured them by the ties of our common kindred to disavow these usurpations, which, would inevitably interrupt our connections and correspondence. They too have been deaf to the voice of justice and of consanguinity. We must, therefore, acquiesce in the necessity, which denounces our Separation, and hold them, as we hold the rest of mankind, Enemies in War, in Peace Friends.

We, therefore, the Representatives of the united States of America, in General Congress, Assembled, appealing to the Supreme Judge of the world for the rectitude of our intentions, do, in the Name, and by Authority of the good People of these Colonies, solemnly publish and declare, That these United Colonies are, and of Right ought to be free and independent states; that they are Absolved from all Allegiance to the British Crown, and that all political connection between them and the State of Great Britain, is and ought to be totally dissolved; and that as Free and Independent States, they have full Power to levy War, conclude Peace, contract Alliances, establish Commerce, and to do all other Acts and Things which Independent States may of right do. And for the support of this Declaration, with a firm reliance on the protection of divine Providence, we mutually pledge to each other our Lives, our Fortunes and our sacred Honor.

[Signed by] John Hancock [President]

Georgia:
Button Gwinnett
Lyman Hall
George Walton

New Hampshire:
Josiah Bartlett
William Whipple
Matthew Thornton

North Carolina:
Wm. Hooper
Joseph Hewes
John Penn

South Carolina:
Edward Rutledge
Thomas Hayward, Jr.
Thomas Lynch, Jr.
Arthur Middleton

Maryland:
Samuel Chase
William Paca
Thomas Stone
Charles Carroll of
    Carrollton

Virginia:
George Wythe

Richard Henry Lee
Thomas Jefferson
Benjamin Harrison
Thomas Nelson, Jr.
Francis Lightfoot Lee
Carter Braxton

Pennsylvania:
Robert Morris
Benjamin Rush
Benjamin Franklin
John Morton
George Clymer
Jason Smith
George Taylor
James Wilson
George Ross

Delaware:
Caesar Rodney
George Read
Thomas M'Kean

New York:
William Floyd
Phillip Livingston
Francis Lewis
Lewis Morris

New Jersey:
Richard Stockton
John Witherspoon
Francis Hopkinson
John Hart
Abraham Clark

Massachusetts:
Samuel Adams
John Adams
Robert Treatpaine

Elbridge Gerry

Rhode Island:
Stephen Hopkins
William Ellery

Connecticut:
Roger Sherman
Samuel Huntington
William Williams
Oliver Wolcott

Mr. Ferdinand Jefferson, Keeper of the Rolls in the Department of State, at Washington, says: "The names of the signers are spelt above as in the facsimile of the original, but the punctuation of them is not always the same; neither do the names of the States appear in the facsimile of the original. The names of the signers of each State are grouped together in the facsimile of the original, except the name of Matthew Thornton, which follows that of Oliver Wolcott."—Revised Statutes of the United States, 2nd ed., 1878.

---

www.archives.gov/exhibits/charters/declaration_transcript.html. Accessed February 17, 2010.

9. BENJAMIN RUSH OPPOSES PRICE CONTROLS

War is expensive, as the Revolutionaries soon found out. By 1776 there was a crisis of currency, and the concern of many was that unless prices and wages were somehow held steady, and profiteering controlled, runaway inflation would jeopardize the ability to fund the military. Wage and price controls were recommended and adopted individually by a few New England states. In February 1777, Congress heatedly debated the measure, and Dr. Benjamin Rush registered his opposition.

Upon the question whether the Congress should recommend to the States to adopt the plan for reducing and regulating the price of labor, manufactures, imports, and provisions, which had been adopted in the four New England States: . . .

Dr Rush: I am against the whole of the resolution. It is founded in the contrary of justice—policy & necessity as has been declared in the resolution. The wisdom & power of government have been employed in all ages to regulate the price of necessaries to no purpose. It was attempted in England in the reign of Edward II by the English parliament, but without effect. The laws for limiting the price of every thing were repealed, and Mr Hume, who mentions this fact, records even the very attempt as a monument of human folly.

The Congress with all its authority have failed in a former instance of regulating the price of goods. You have limited Bohea tea to ¾ of a dollar, and yet it is daily sold before your eyes for 30/. The committee of Philadelphia limited the price of West India goods about a year ago—But what was the consequence? The merchants it is true sold their rum, sugar & molasses at the price limited by the committee, but they charged a heavy profit upon the barrel or the paper which contained the rum or the sugar.

Consider, Sir, the danger of failing in this experiment.

The Salvation of this continent depends upon the authority of this Congress being held as sacred as the cause of liberty itself. Suppose we should fail of producing the effects we wish for by the resolution before you. Have we any character to spare? Have we committed no mistakes in the management of the public affairs of America? We have, sir! It becomes us therefore, to be careful of the remains of our Authority & character.

It is a common thing to cry aloud of the rapacity & extortion in every branch of business & among every class of men. This has led some people to decry the *public virtue* of this country. True Sir, there is not so much of it as we could wish, but there is much more that is sometimes allowed on this floor. We estimate our virtue by a false barometer, when we measure it by the price of goods. The extortion we complain off arises only from the excessive quantity of our money. Now, Sir, a failure in this attempt to regulate the price of goods will encrease the clamors against the rapacity of dealers, and thus depreciate our public virtue.

Consider, Sir, the consequence of measuring our virtue by this false standard. You will add weight to the arguments used at St. James's to explode patriotism altogether, & by denying its existence in this country, destroy it forever. Persuade a woman that there is no such thing as chastity, & if there is that, she does not possess it, and she may be easily seduced if she was as chaste as Diana. Sir, The price of goods may be compared to a number of light substances in a bason of water. The hand may keep them down for a while, but nothing can detain them on the bottom of the bason but an abstraction of the water. The continent labours under a universal malady.

From the crown of her head to the Soal of her feet she is full of disorders. She requires the most powerful tonic medicines. The resolution before you is nothing but an *opiate*. It may compose the continent for a night, but she will soon awaken again to a fresh sense of her pain & misery.

The Pennsylvania Magazine of History and Biography, vol. 27 (Philadelphia: Historical Society of Pennsylvania).

10. LETTER FROM ABIGAIL TO JOHN ADAMS, BOSTON, JULY 31, 1777

In a letter to her husband, Abigail Adams reported on the ladies of Boston throwing a tea party of their own.

There is a great scarcity of sugar and coffee,—articles which the female part of the State is very loath to give up, especially whilst they consider the scarcity occasioned by the merchants having secreted a large quantity. There had been much rout and noise in the town for several weeks. Some stores had been opened by a number of people, and the coffee and sugar carried into the market and dealt out by pounds. It was rumored that an eminent, wealthy, stingy merchant (who is a bachelor) had a hogshead of coffee in his store, which he refused to sell the committee under six shillings per pound. A number of females—some say a hundred, some say more—assembled with a cart and trucks, marched down to the warehouse, and demanded the keys, which he refused to deliver. Upon which one of them seized him by his neck and tossed him into the cart. Upon his finding no quarter, he delivered the keys, when they tipped up the cart and discharged him; then opened the warehouse, hoisted out the coffee themselves, put it into the trunks, and drove off. It was reported that he had personal chastisements among them; but this I believe was not true. A large concourse of men stood amazed, silent spectators of the whole transaction!"

Justin Winsor, *The Memorial History of Boston, Including Suffolk County*, vol. 4 (Boston: Ticknor and Co., 1886).

11. PAUL REVERE'S FAMOUS RIDE, IN HIS OWN WORDS

In this letter to Rev. Jeremy Belknap, the founder of the Massachusetts Historical Society, Revere related the events that led up to his famous ride to Lexington. He also discussed his work as a spy and the double agent in the camp who betrayed the Patriots.

DEAR SIR,—Having a little leisure, I wish to fulfil my promise of giving you some facts and anecdotes prior to the battle of Lexington, which I do not remember to have seen in any History of the American Revolution.

In the year 1773, I was employed by the Selectmen of the town of Boston to carry the account of the Destruction of the Tea to New York; and afterwards, 1774, to carry their despatches to New York and Philadelphia for calling a Congress; and afterwards to Congress several times. In the fall of 1774 and winter of 1775, I was one of upwards of thirty, chiefly mechanics, who formed ourselves into a committee for the purpose of watching the movements of the British soldiers, and gaining every intelligence of the movements of the Tories. We held our meetings at the Green Dragon tavern. We were so careful that our meetings should be kept secret, that every time we met every person swore upon the Bible that they would not discover any of our transactions but to Messrs. Hancock, Adams, Doctors Warren, Church, and one or two more.

About November, when things began to grow serious, a gentleman who had connections with the Tory party, but was a Whig at heart, acquainted me, that our meetings were discovered, and mentioned the identical words that were spoken among us the night before. We did not then distrust Dr. Church, but supposed it must be some one among us. We removed to another place, which we thought was more secure; but here we found that all our transactions were communicated to Governor Gage. (This came to me through the then Secretary Flucker; he told it to the gentleman mentioned above.) It was then a common opinion, that there was a traitor in the Provincial Congress, and that Gage was possessed of all their secrets. (Church was a member of that Congress for Boston.) In the winter, towards the spring, we frequently took turns, two and two, to watch the soldiers, by patrolling the streets all night. The Saturday night preceding the 19th of April, about 12 o'clock at night, the boats belonging to the transports were all launched, and carried under the sterns of the men-of-war. (They had been previously hauled up and repaired.) We likewise found that the grenadiers and light infantry were all taken off duty.

From these movements, we expected something serious was to be transacted. On Tuesday evening, the 18th, it was observed that a number of soldiers were marching towards the bottom of the Common. About 10 o'clock, Dr. Warren sent in great haste for me, and begged that I would immediately set off for Lexington, where Messrs. Hancock and Adams were, and acquaint them of the movement, and that it was thought they were the objects. When I got to Dr. Warren's house, I found he had sent an express by land to Lexington,—a Mr. William Dawes. The Sunday before, by desire of Dr. Warren, I had been to Lexington, to Messrs. Hancock and Adams, who were at the Rev. Mr. Clark's. I returned at night through Charlestown; there I agreed with a Colonel Conant and some other gentlemen, that if the British went out by water, we would show two lanthorns in the North Church steeple; and if by land, one, as a signal; for we were apprehensive it would be difficult to cross the Charles River, or get over Boston Neck. I left Dr. Warren, called upon a friend, and desired him to make the signals. I then went home, took my boots and surtout, went to the north part of the town, where I had kept a boat; two friends rowed me across Charles River, a little to the eastward where the Somerset man-of-war lay. It was then young flood, the ship was winding, and the moon was rising. They landed me on the Charlestown side. When I got into town, I met Colonel Conant, and several others; they said they had seen our signals. I told them what was acting, and went to get me a horse; I got a horse of Deacon Larkin. While the horse was preparing, Richard Devens, Esq., who was one of the Committee of Safety, came to me, and told me that he came down the road from Lexington, after sun-down, that evening; that he met ten British officers, all well mounted, and armed, going up the road.

I set off upon a very good horse; it was then about eleven o'clock, and very pleasant. After I had passed Charlestown Neck, and got nearly opposite where Mark was hung in chains, I saw two men on horseback, under a tree. When I got near them, I discovered they were British officers. One tried to get ahead of me, and the other to take me. I turned my horse very quick, and galloped towards Charlestown Neck, and then pushed for the Medford road. The one who chased me, endeavoring to cut me off, got into a clay pond, near where the new tavern is now built. I got clear of him, and went through Medford, over the bridge, and up to Menotomy. In Medford, I awaked the Captain of the min-ute men; and after that, I alarmed almost every house, till I got to Lexington. I found Messrs. Hancock and Adams at the Rev. Mr. Clark's; I told them my errand, and inquired for Mr. Dawes; they said he had not been there; I related the story of the two officers, and supposed that he must have been stopped, as he ought to have been there before me. After I had been there about half an hour, Mr. Dawes came; we refreshed ourselves, and set off for Concord, to secure the stores, &c. there. We were overtaken by a young Dr. Precot, whom we found to be a high Son of Liberty. I told them of the ten officers that Mr. Devens met, and that it was prob-able we might be stopped before we got to Concord; for I supposed that after night, they divided themselves, and that two of them had fixed themselves in such passages as were most likely to stop any intelligence going to Concord. I likewise mentioned that we had better alarm all the inhabitants till we got to Concord; the young Doctor much approved of it, and said he would stop with either of us, for the people between that and Concord knew him, and would give the more credit to what we said. We had got nearly half way: Mr. Dawes and the Doctor stopped to alarm the people of a house: I was about one hundred rods ahead, when I saw two men, in nearly the same situation as those officers were, near Charlestown. I called for the Doctor and Mr. Dawes to come up; in an instant I was surrounded by four;—they had placed themselves in a straight road, that inclined each way; they had taken down a pair of bars on the north side of the road, and two of them were under a tree in the pasture. The Doctor being foremost, he came up; and we tried to get past them; but they being armed with pistols and swords, they forced us into the pasture;—the Doctor jumped his horse over a low stone wall, and got to Concord. I observed a wood at a small distance, and made for that. When I got there, out started six officers, on horseback, and ordered me to dismount;—one of them, who appeared to have the command, examined me, where I came from, and what my name was? I told him. He asked me if I was an express? I answered in the affirmative. He demanded what time I left Boston? I told him; and added, that their troops had catched aground in passing the river, and that there would be five hundred Americans there in a short time, for I had alarmed the country all the way up. He immediately rode towards those who stopped us, when all five of them came down upon a full gallop; one of them, whom I afterwards found to be a Major Mitchel, of the 5th Regiment, clapped his pistol to my head, called me by name, and told me he was going to ask me some questions, and if I did not give him true answers, he would blow my brains out. He then asked me similar questions to those above. He then ordered me to mount my horse, after searching me for arms. He then ordered them to advance, and to lead me in front. When we got to the road, they turned down towards Lexington. When we had got about one mile, the Major rode up to the officer that was leading me, and told him to give me to the Sergeant. As soon as he took me, the Major ordered him, if I attempted to run, or anybody insulted them, to blow my brains out. We rode till we got near Lexington meeting-house, when the militia fired a volley of guns, which appeared to alarm them very much. The Major inquired of me how far it was to Cambridge, and if there were any other road? After some consultation, the Major rode up to the Sergeant, and asked if his horse was tired? He answered him, he was—(he was a Sergeant of Grenadiers, and had a small horse)—then, said he, take that man's horse. I dismounted, and the Sergeant mounted my horse, when they all rode towards Lexington meeting-house. I went across the burying-ground, and some pastures, and came to the Rev. Mr. Clark's house, where I found Messrs. Hancock and Adams. I told them of my treatment, and they concluded to go from that house towards Woburn. I went with them, and a Mr. Lowell, who was a clerk to Mr. Hancock. When we got to the house where they intended to stop, Mr. Lowell and myself returned to Mr. Clark's, to find what was going on. When we got there, an elderly man came in; he said he had just come from the tavern, that a man had come from Boston, who said there were no British troops coming. Mr. Lowell and myself went towards the tavern, when we met a man on a full gallop, who told us the troops were coming up the rocks. We afterwards met another, who said they were close by. Mr. Lowell asked me to go to the tavern with him, to get a trunk of papers belonging to Mr. Hancock. We went up chamber; and while we were getting the trunk, we saw the British very near, upon a full march. We hurried towards Mr. Clark's house. In our way, we passed through the militia. There were about fifty. When we had got about one hundred yards from the meeting-house, the British troops appeared on both sides of the meeting-house. In their front was an officer on horseback. They made a short halt; *when I saw, and heard, a gun fired*, which appeared to be a pistol. Then I could distinguish two guns, and then a continual roar of musketry; when we made off with the trunk.

As I have mentioned Dr. Church, perhaps it might not be disagreeable to mention some matters of my own knowledge, respecting him. He appeared to be a high Son of Liberty. He frequented all the places where they met, was encouraged by all the leaders of the Sons of Liberty, and it appeared he was respected by them, though I knew that Dr. Warren had not the greatest affection for him. He was esteemed a very capable writer, especially in verse; and as the Whig party needed every strength, they feared, as well as courted him. Though it was known that some of the liberty songs, which he composed, were parodized by him, in favor of the British, yet none dare charge him with it. I was a constant and critical observer of him, and I must say, that I never thought him a man of principle; and I doubted much in my own mind whether he was a real Whig. I knew that he kept company with a Capt. Price, a half-pay British officer, and that he frequently dined with him, and Robinson, one of the Commissioners. I know that one of his intimate acquaintance asked him why he was so often with Robinson and Price? His answer was, that he kept company with them on purpose to find out their plans. The day after the battle of Lexington, I met him in Cambridge, when he shew me some blood on his stocking, which he said spirted on him from a man who was killed near him, as he was urging the militia on. I well remember, that I argued with myself, if a man will risk his life in a cause, he must be a friend to that cause; and I never suspected him after, till he was charged with being a traitor.

The same day I met Dr. Warren. He was President of the Committee of Safety. He engaged me as a messenger, to do the out of doors business for that committee: which gave me an opportunity of being frequently with them. The Friday evening after, about sunset, I was sitting with some, or near all that committee, in their room, which was at Mr. Hastings's house in Cambridge. Dr. Church, all at once, started up—Dr. Warren, said he, I am determined to go into Boston to-mor-row—(it set them all a staring)—Dr. Warren replied, Are you serious, Dr. Church? they will hang you if they catch you in Boston. He replied, I am serious, and am determined to go at all adventures. After a considerable conversation, Dr. Warren said, If you are determined, let us make some business for you. They agreed that he should go to get medicine for their and our wounded officers. He went the next morning; and I think he came back on Sunday evening. After he had told the committee how things were, I took him aside and inquired particularly how they treated him. He said, that as soon as he got to their lines, on Boston Neck, they made him a prisoner, and carried him to General Gage, where he was examined, and then he was sent to Gould's barracks, and was not suffered to go home but once. After he was taken up, for holding a correspondence with the British, I came across Deacon Caleb Davis;—we entered into conversation about him;—he told me, that the morning Church went into Boston, he (Davis) received a billet for General Gage—(he then did not know that Church was in town)—when he got to the General's house, he was told, the General could not be spoke with, that he was in private with a gentleman; that he waited near half an hour, when General Gage and Dr. Church came out of a room, discoursing together, like persons who had been long acquainted. He appeared to be quite surprised at seeing Deacon Davis there; that he (Church) went where he pleased, while in Boston, only a Major Caine, one of Gage's Aids, went with him. I was told by another person, whom I could depend upon, that he saw Church go into General Gage's house, at the above time; that he got out of the chaise and went up the steps more like a man that was acquainted than a prisoner.

Some time after, perhaps a year or two, I fell in company with a gentleman who studied with Church; in discoursing about him, I related what I have mentioned above; he said, he did not doubt that he was in the interest of the British; and that it was he who informed General Gage; that he knew for certain, that a short time before the battle of Lexington, (for he then lived with him, and took care of his business and books), he had no money by him, and was much drove for money; that all at once, he had several hundred new British guineas; and that he thought at the time, where they came from.

Thus, Sir, I have endeavored to give you a short detail of some matters, of which perhaps no person but myself has documents or knowledge. I have mentioned some names which you are acquainted with; I wish you would ask them, if they can remember the circumstance I allude to.

I am, Sir, with every sentiment of esteem, your humble servant,

—Paul Revere

Elbridge Henry Goss, *The Life of Colonel Paul Revere*, vol. 1 (Boston: Joseph George Cupples, 1891).

12. Thomas Jefferson on Passing the Declaration of Independence

Thomas Jefferson related the heated debates on independence, the frustrating obstinance of some of the delegates at the Continental Congress, the writing and repeated editing of his draft of the Declaration of Independence, and finally—victory: On July 4th of 1776, twelve of the thirteen colonies reached agreement to formally proclaim themselves as a free and independent nation. (New York added its support on July 9 by proclamation.)

It appearing in the course of these debates [on a motion of the Virginia delegates declaring the colonies independent of Great Britain] that the colonies of N. York, New Jersey, Pennsylvania, Delaware, Maryland, and South Carolina were not yet matured for falling from the parent stem, but that they were fast advancing to that state, it was thought most prudent to wait a while for them, and to postpone the final decision to July 1. but that this might occasion as little delay as possible a committee was appointed to prepare a declaration of independence. The commee were J. Adams, Dr. Franklin, Roger Sherman, Robert R. Livingston & myself. Committees were also appointed at the same time to prepare a plan of confederation for the colonies, and to state the terms proper to be proposed for foreign alliance. The committee for drawing the declaration of Independence desired me to do it. It was accordingly done, and being approved by them, I reported it to the house on Friday the 28th of June when it was read and ordered to lie on the table. On Monday, the 1st of July the house resolved itself into a commee of the whole & resumed the consideration of the original motion made by the delegates of Virginia, which being again debated through the day, was carried in the affirmative by the votes of N. Hampshire, Connecticut, Massachusetts, Rhode Island, N. Jersey, Maryland, Virginia, N. Carolina, & Georgia. S. Carolina and Pennsylvania voted against it. Delaware having but two members present, they were divided. The delegates for New York declared they were for it themselves & were assured their constituents were for it, but that their instructions having been drawn near a twelvemonth before, when reconciliation was still the general object, they were enjoined by them to do nothing which should impede that object. They therefore thought themselves not justifiable in voting on either side, and asked leave to withdraw from the question, which was given them. The commee rose & reported their resolution to the house. Mr. Edward Rutledge of S. Carolina then requested the determination might be put off to the next day, as he believed his colleagues, tho' they disapproved of the resolution, would then join in it for the sake of unanimity. The ultimate question whether the house would agree to the resolution of the committee was accordingly postponed to the next day, when it was again moved and S. Carolina concurred in voting for it. In the meantime a third member had come post from the Delaware counties and turned the vote of that colony in favour of the resolution. Members of a different sentiment attending that morning from Pennsylvania also, their vote was changed, so that the whole 12 colonies who were authorized to vote at all, gave their voices for it; and within a few days, the convention of N. York approved of it and thus supplied the void occasioned by the withdrawing of her delegates from the vote.

Congress proceeded the same day to consider the declaration of Independence which had been reported & lain on the table the Friday preceding, and on Monday referred to a commee of the whole. The pusillanimous idea that we had friends in England worth keeping terms with, still haunted the minds of many. For this reason those passages which conveyed censures on the people of England were struck out, lest they should give them offence. The clause too, reprobating the enslaving the inhabitants of Africa, was struck out in complaisance to South Carolina and Georgia, who had never attempted to restrain the importation of slaves, and who on the contrary still wished to continue it. Our northern brethren also I believe felt a little tender under those censures; for tho' their people have very few slaves themselves yet they had been pretty considerable carriers of them to others. The debates having taken up the greater parts of the 2d 3d & 4th days of July were, in the evening of the last, closed the declaration was reported by the commee, agreed to by the house and signed by every member present except Mr. Dickinson.

William B. Cairns, ed., *Selections from Early American Writers: 1607–1800* (New York: Macmillan, 1909).

13. GENERAL HULL ON THE KILLING OF HIS FRIEND NATHAN HALE

Nathan Hale (1755–1776) was just a schoolteacher in his twenties when war broke out. Commissioned as a lieutenant in the colonial army, in September of 1776, he volunteered for a dangerous mission: disguised as a schoolmaster, he would sneak behind British lines in New York to gather intelligence. Unfortunately for the young patriot, he was discovered, interrogated, and executed without a trial. Captain William Hull of the Continental army wrote this moving report of Hale's last day and his enduring final words.

There was no young man who gave fairer promise of an enlightened and devoted service to his country, than this my friend and companion in arms. His naturally fine intellect had been carefully cultivated, and his heart was filled with generous emotions; but, like the soaring eagle, the patriotic ardour of his soul "winged the dart which caused his destruction."

After his interview with Colonel Knowlton, he repaired to my quarters, and informed me of what had passed. He remarked, "That he thought he owed to his country the accomplishment of an object so important, and so much desired by the Commander of her armies, and he knew of no other mode of obtaining the information, than by assuming a disguise and passing into the enemy's camp." He asked my candid opinion. I replied, that it was an action which involved serious consequences, and the propriety of it was doubtful; and though *he* viewed the business of a spy as a *duty*, yet, he could not officially be required to perform it. That such a service was not claimed of the meanest soldier, though many might be willing, for a pecuniary compensation, to engage in it; and as for himself, the employment was not in keeping with his character. His nature was too frank and open for deceit and disguise, and he was incapable of acting a part equally foreign to his feelings and habits. Admitting that he was successful, who would wish success at such a price? Did his country demand the moral degradation of her sons, to advance her interests? Stratagems are resorted to in war; they are feints and evasions, performed under no disguise; are familiar to commanders; form a part of their plans, and, considered in a military view, lawful and advantageous. The tact with which they are executed, exacts admiration from the enemy. But who respects the character of a spy, assuming the garb of friendship but to betray? The very death assigned him is expressive of the estimation in which he is held. As soldiers, let us do our duty in the field; contend for our legitimate rights, and not stain our honour by the sacrifice of integrity. And when present events, with all their deep and exciting interests, shall have passed away, may the blush of shame never arise, by the remembrance of an unworthy, though successful act, in the performance of which we were deceived by the belief that it was sanctified by its object. I ended by saying, that should he undertake the enterprise, his short, bright career, would close with an ignominious death.

He replied, "I am fully sensible of the consequences of discovery and capture in such a situation. But for a year I have been attached to the army, and have not rendered any material service, while receiving a compensation, for which I make no return. Yet," he continued, "I am not influenced by the expectation of promotion or pecuniary reward; I wish to be useful, and every kind of service, necessary to the public good, becomes honourable by being necessary. If the exigencies of my country demand a peculiar service, its claims to perform that service are imperious."

He spoke with warmth and decision. I replied, "That such are your wishes, cannot be doubted. But is this the most effectual mode of carrying them into execution? In the progress of the war, there will be ample opportunity to give your talents and your life, should it be so ordered, to the sacred cause to which we are pledged. You can bestow upon your country the richest benefits, and win for yourself the highest honours. Your exertions for her interests will be daily felt, while, by one fatal act, you crush for ever the power and the opportunity Heaven offers, for her glory and your happiness."

I urged him, for the love of country, for the love of kindred, to abandon an enterprise which would only end in the sacrifice of the dearest interests of both.

He paused—then affectionately taking my hand, he said, "I will reflect, and do nothing but what duty demands." He was absent from the army, and I feared he had gone to the British lines, to execute his fatal purpose. In a few days an officer came to our camp, under a flag of truce, and informed Hamilton, then a captain of artillery, but afterwards the aid of General Washington, that Captain Hale had been arrested within the British lines, condemned as a spy, and executed that morning.

I learned the melancholy particulars from this officer, who was present at his execution, and seemed touched by the circumstances attending it.

He said that Captain Hale had passed through their army, both of Long Island and York Island. That he had procured sketches of the fortifications, and made memoranda of their number and different positions. When apprehended, he was taken before Sir William Howe, and these papers, found concealed about his person, betrayed his intentions. He at once declared his name, his rank in the American army, and his object in coming within the British lines.

Sir William Howe, without the form of a trial, gave orders for his execution the following morning. He was placed in the custody of the Provost Marshal, who was a Refugee, and hardened to human suffering and every softening sentiment of the heart. Captain Hale, alone, without sympathy or support, save that from above, on the near approach of death asked for a clergyman to attend him. It was refused. He then requested a Bible; that too was refused by his inhuman jailer.

"On the morning of his execution," continued the officer, "my station was near the fatal spot, and I requested the Provost Marshal to permit the prisoner to sit in my marquee, while he was making the necessary preparations. Captain Hale entered: he was calm, and bore himself with gentle dignity, in the consciousness of rectitude and high intentions. He asked for writing materials, which I furnished him: he wrote two letters, one to his mother and one to a brother officer." He was shortly after summoned to the gallows. But a few persons were around him, yet his characteristic dying words were remembered. He said, 'I only regret, that I have but one life to lose for my country.'"

Thus terminated the earthly existence of a man, whose country mourned the loss of one of her fairest sons, and whose friends wept, in the bitter recollection of his untimely fate.

The Provost Marshal, in the diabolical spirit of cruelty, destroyed the letters of his prisoner, and assigned as a reason, "that the rebels should not know that they had a man in their army who could die with so much firmness."

Maria Campbell, ed., *Revolutionary and Civil Life of General William Hull* (Boston: Appleton, 1846).

14. THOMAS PAINE'S COMMON SENSE
(SELECTIONS)

Published anonymously by Thomas Paine in 1776, Common
Sense—*using plain language everyone could understand—
became one of the most influential writings of the American
Revolution. It advocated a declaration of independence from Great
Britain and stirred the pot of rising revolutionary sentiment.*

Some writers have so confounded society with government,
as to leave little or no distinction between them; whereas they
are not only different, but have different origins. Society is
produced by our wants, and government by our wickedness;
the former promotes our happiness *positively*, by uniting our
affections; the latter *negatively*, by restraining our vices. The
one encourages intercourse, the other creates distinctions.
The first is a patron, the last is a punisher.

Society in every state is a blessing, but government, even
in its best state, is but a necessary evil; in its worst state, an
intolerable one; for when we suffer, or are exposed to the same
miseries *by a government*, which we might expect in a country
without government, our calamity is heightened by reflecting
that we furnish the means by which we suffer. Government,
like dress, is the badge of lost innocence: the palaces of kings
are built on the ruins of the bowers of paradise. For, were
the impulses of conscience clear, uniform, and irresistibly
obeyed, man would need no other lawgiver; but that not
being the case, he finds it necessary to surrender up a part of
his property to furnish means for the protection of the rest;

and this he is induced to do by the same prudence which, in every other case, advises him out of two evils to choose the least. *Wherefore*, security being the true design and end of government, it unanswerably follows, that whatever *form* thereof appears most likely to ensure it to us with the least expense and greatest benefit, is preferable to all others. . . .

Oppression is often the *consequence*, but seldom or never the *means* of riches; and though avarice will preserve a man from being necessitously poor, it generally makes him too timorous to be wealthy.

But there is another and greater distinction, for which no truly natural or religious reason can be assigned, and that is, the distinction of men into KINGS and SUBJECTS. Male and female are the distinctions of nature, good and bad the distinctions of heaven; but how a race of men came into the world so exalted above the rest, and distinguished like some new species, is worth enquiring into, and whether they are the means of happiness or of misery to mankind. . . .

One of the strongest *natural* proofs of the folly of hereditary right of kings, is that nature disapproves it, otherwise she would not so frequently turn it into ridicule by giving mankind *an ass for a lion.* . . .

Every quiet method for peace hath been ineffectual. Our prayers have been rejected with disdain; and only tended to convince us that nothing flatters vanity, or confirms obstinacy in kings more than repeated petitioning—and nothing hath contributed more than this very measure to make the kings of Europe absolute. . . .

As to government matters, it is not in the power of

Britain to do this continent justice: the business of it will soon be too weighty and intricate to be managed with any tolerable degree of convenience, by a power so distant from us, and so very ignorant of us; for if they cannot conquer us, they cannot govern us. . . .

O ye that love mankind! Ye that dare oppose, not only the tyranny, but the tyrant, stand forth! Every spot of the old world is overrun with oppression. Freedom hath been hunted round the globe. Asia and Africa have long expelled her, Europe regards her like a stranger, and England hath given her warning to depart. O! receive the fugitive, and prepare in time an asylum for mankind. . . .

Since the publication of the first edition of this pamphlet, or rather, on the same day on which it came out, the king's speech made its appearance in this city [Philadelphia]. Had the spirit of prophecy directed the birth of this production, it could not have brought it forth at a more seasonable juncture, or at a more necessary time. The bloody-mindedness of the one, shows the necessity of pursuing the doctrine of the other. Men read by way of revenge: and the speech, instead of terrifying, prepared a way for the manly principles of independence.

Thomas Paine, *Common Sense* (New York: Peter Eckler, 1918).

15. THE ARTICLES OF CONFEDERATION (1777)

The Articles of Confederation and Perpetual Union were adopted in the heat of the Revolutionary War by the Continental Congress in 1777, and they took effect in 1781. The Articles established a framework that legally established the union of the states while allowing each state to retain its sovereignty. Although Congress was given the power to declare war and to maintain an army and navy, it lacked the authority to set up tariffs, regulate commerce, and levy taxes. The Articles were replaced by the U.S. Constitution on June 21, 1788.

To all to whom these Presents shall come, we, the undersigned, Delegates of the States affixed to our Names, send greeting: Whereas the Delegates of the United States of America in Congress assembled, did on the fifteenth day of November, in the year of our Lord one thousand seven hundred and seventy seven, and in the second year of the Independence of America, agree to certain articles of Confederation and perpetual Union between the states of New Hampshire, Massachusetts-bay, Rhode Island and Providence Plantations, Connecticut, New York, New Jersey, Pennsylvania, Delaware, Maryland, Virginia, North Carolina, South Carolina, and Georgia, in the words following, viz. Articles of Confederation and perpetual Union between the States of New Hampshire, Massachusetts-bay, Rhode Island and Providence Plantations, Connecticut, New York, New Jersey, Pennsyl-vania, Delaware, Maryland, Virginia, North Carolina, South Carolina, and Georgia.

ARTICLE I.

The stile of this confederacy shall be, "The United States of America."

ARTICLE II.

Each State retains its sovereignty, freedom, and independence, and every power, jurisdiction, and right, which is not by this confederation, expressly delegated to the United States, in Congress assembled.

ARTICLE III.

The said States hereby severally enter into a firm league of friendship with each other, for their common defence, the security of their liberties, and their mutual and general welfare, binding themselves to assist each other against all force offered to, or attacks made upon them, or any of them, on account of religion, sovereignty, trade, or any other pretense whatever.

ARTICLE IV.

The better to secure and perpetuate mutual friendship and intercourse among the people of the different States in this union, the free inhabitants of each of these States, paupers, vagabonds, and fugitives from justice excepted, shall be entitled to all privileges and immunities of free citizens in the several States; and the people of each State shall free ingress and regress to and from any other State, and shall enjoy therein all the privileges of trade and commerce, subject to the same duties, impositions, and restrictions, as the inhabitants thereof respectively; provided that such restrictions shall not extend so far as to prevent the removal of property imported into any State, to any other State, of which the owner is an inhabitant; provided also, that no imposition, duties, or restriction, shall be laid by any State on the property of the United States, or either of them.

If any person guilty of, or charged with, treason, felony, or other high misdemeanor in any State, shall flee from justice, and be found in any of the united States, he shall, upon demand of the governor or executive power of the State from which he fled, be delivered up, and removed to the State having jurisdiction of his offense.

Full faith and credit shall be given, in each of these States, to the records, acts, and judicial proceedings of the courts and magistrates of every other State.

ARTICLE V.

For the most convenient management of the general interests of the united States, delegates shall be annually appointed in such manner as the legislatures of each State shall direct, to meet in Congress on the first Monday in November, in every year, with a power reserved to each State to recall its delegates, or any of them, at any time within the year, and to send others in their stead, for the remainder of the year.

No State shall be represented in Congress by less than two, nor by more than Seven Members; and no person shall be capable of being delegate for more than three years, in any term of Six years; nor shall any person, being a delegate, be capable of holding any office under the united States, for which he, or another for his benefit, receives any salary, fees, or emolument of any kind.

Each State shall maintain its own delegates in a meeting of the States, and while they act as members of the committee of the States.

In determining questions in the united States in Congress assembled, each State shall have one vote.

Freedom of speech and debate in Congress shall not be impeached or questioned in any Court or place out of Congress; and the members of Congress shall be protected in their persons from arrests or imprisonments during the time of their going to and from, and attendence on, Congress, except for treason, felony or breach of the peace.

ARTICLE VI.

No State, without the consent of the united States, in congress assembled, shall send any embassy to, or receive any embassy from, or enter into any conference, agreement, alliance, or treaty, with any King, prince or State; nor shall any person holding any office of profit or trust under the united States, or any of them, accept of any present, emolument, office, or title of any kind whatever, from any king, prince, or foreign State; nor shall the united States, in congress assembled, or any of them, grant any title of nobility.

No two or more States shall enter into any treaty, confederation, or alliance whatever, between them, without the consent of the united States, in Congress assembled, specifying accurately the purposes for which the same is to be entered into, and how long it shall continue.

No State shall lay any imposts or duties, which may interfere with any stipulations in treaties, entered into by the united States, in congress assembled, with any king, prince, or State, in pursuance of any treaties already proposed by congress to the courts of France and Spain.

No vessels of war shall be kept up in time of peace, by any State, except such number only as shall be deemed necessary by the united States, in congress assembled, for the defense of such State, or its trade; nor shall any body of forces be kept up, by any State, in time of peace, except such number only as, in the judgment of the united States, in congress assembled, shall be deemed requisite to garrison the forts necessary for the defence of such State; but every State shall always keep up a well-regulated and disciplined militia, sufficiently armed and accounted, and shall provide and constantly have ready for use, in public stores, a due number of field-pieces and tents, and a proper quantity of arms, ammunition, and camp equipage.

No State shall engage in any war without the consent of the united States, in congress assembled, unless such State be actually invaded by enemies, or shall have received certain advice of a resolution being formed by some nation of Indians to invade such State, and the danger is so imminent as not to admit of a delay till the united States, in congress assembled can be consulted; nor shall any State grant commissions to any ships or vessels of war, nor letters of marque or reprisal, except it be after a declaration of war by the united States, in congress assembled, and then only against the kingdom or State, and the subjects thereof, against which war has been so declared, and under such regulations as shall be established by the united States, in congress assembled, unless such State be infested by pirates, in which case vessels of war may be fitted out for that occasion, and kept so long as the danger shall continue, or until the united States, in congress assembled, shall determine otherwise.

ARTICLE VII.

When land forces are raised by any State, for the common defence, all officers of or under the rank of colonel, shall be appointed by the legislature of each State respectively by whom such forces shall be raised, or in such manner as such State shall direct, and all vacancies shall be filled up by the State which first made appointment.

ARTICLE VIII.

All charges of war, and all other expenses that shall be incurred for the common defence or general welfare, and allowed by the united States, in congress assembled, shall be defrayed out of a common treasury, which shall be supplied by the several States, in proportion to the value of all land within each State, granted to or surveyed for, any person, as such land and the buildings and improvements thereon shall be estimated, according to such mode as the united States, in congress assembled, shall, from time to time, direct and appoint. The taxes for paying that proportion shall be laid and levied by the authority and direction of the legislatures of the several States, within the time agreed upon by the united States, in congress assembled.

ARTICLE IX.

The united States, in congress assembled, shall have the sole and exclusive right and power of determining on peace and war, except in the cases mentioned in the sixth Article, of sending and receiving ambassadors; entering into treaties and alliances, provided that no treaty of commerce shall be made, whereby the legislative power of the respective States shall be restrained from imposing such imposts and duties on foreigners, as their own people are subjected to, or from prohibiting the exportation or importation of any species of goods or commodities whatsoever; of establishing rules for deciding, in all cases, what captures on land or water shall be legal, and in what manner prizes taken by land or naval forces in the service of the united States, shall be divided or appropriated; of granting letters of marque and reprisal in times of peace; appointing courts for the trial of piracies and felonies commited on the high seas; and establishing courts; for receiving and determineing finally appeals in all cases of captures; provided that no member of congress shall be appointed a judge of any of the said courts.

The united States, in congress assembled, shall also be the last resort on appeal, in all disputes and differences now subsisting, or that hereafter may arise between two or more States concerning boundary, jurisdiction, or any other cause whatever; which authority shall always be exercised in the manner following. Whenever the legislative or executive authority, or lawful agent of any State in controversy with another, shall present a petition to congress, stating the matter in question, and praying for a hearing, notice thereof shall be given, by order of congress, to the legislative or executive authority of the other State in controversy, and a day assigned for the appearance of the parties by their lawful agents, who shall then be directed to appoint, by joint consent, commissioners or judges to constitute a court for hearing and determining the matter in question: but if they cannot agree, congress shall name three persons out of each of the united States, and from the list of such persons each party shall alternately strike out one, the petitioners beginning, until the number shall be reduced to thirteen; and from that number not less than seven, nor more than nine names, as congress shall direct, shall, in the presence of congress, be drawn out by lot, and the persons whose names shall be so drawn, or any five of them, shall be commissioners or judges, to hear and finally determine the controversy, so always as a major part of the judges, who shall hear the cause, shall agree in the determination: and if either party shall neglect to attend at the day appointed, without showing reasons which congress shall judge sufficient, or being present, shall refuse to strike, the congress shall proceed to nominate three persons out of each State, and the secretary of congress shall strike in behalf of such party absent or refusing; and the judgment and sentence of the court, to be appointed in the manner before prescribed, shall be final and conclusive; and if any of the parties shall refuse to submit to the authority of such court, or to appear or defend their claim or cause, the court shall nevertheless proceed to pronounce sentence, or judgment, which shall in like manner be final and decisive; the judgment or sentence and other proceedings being in either case transmitted to congress, and lodged among the acts of congress, for the security of the parties concerned: provided that every commissioner, before he sits in judgement, shall take an oath to be administered by one of the judges of the Supreme or Superior court of the State where the cause shall be tried, "well and truly to hear and determine the matter in question, according to the best of his judgment, without favour, affection, or hope of reward": Provided, also, that no State shall be deprived of territory for the benefit of the united States.

All controversies concerning the private right of soil claimed under different grants of two or more States, whose jurisdictions as they may respect such lands, and the States which passed such grants are adjusted, the said grants or either of them being at the same time claimed to have originated antecedent to such settlement of jurisdiction, shall, on the petition of either party to the congress of the united States, be finally determined, as near as may be, in the same manner as is before presecribed for deciding disputes respecting territorial jurisdiction between different States.

The united States, in congress assembled, shall also have the sole and exclusive right and power of regulating the alloy and value of coin struck by their own authority, or by that of the respective States fixing the standard of weights and measures throughout the united States; regulating the trade and managing all affairs with the Indians, not members of any of the States; provided that the legislative right of any State, within its own limits, be not infringed or violated; establishing and regulating post-offices from one State to another, throughout all the United States, and exacting such postage on the papers passing through the same, as may be requisite to defray the expenses of the said office; appointing all officers of the land forces in the service of the united States, excepting regimental officers; appointing all the officers of the naval forces, and commissioning all officers whatever in the service of the united States; making rules for the government and regulation of the said land and naval forces, and directing their operations.

The united States, in congress assembled shall have authority to appoint a committee, to sit in the recess of congress, to be denominated, "A Committee of the States," and to consist of one delegate from each State; and to appoint such other committees and civil officers as may be necessary for managing the general affairs of the united States under their direction; to appoint one of their number to preside; provided that no person be allowed to serve in the office of president more than one year in any term of three years; to ascertain the necessary sums of money to be raised for the service of the united States, and to appropriate and apply the same for defraying the public expenses; to borrow money or emit bills on the credit of the united States, transmitting every half year to the respective States an account of the sums of money so borrowed or emitted; to build and equip a navy; to agree upon the number of land forces, and to make requisitions from each State for its quota, in proportion to the number of white inhabitants in such State, which requisition shall be binding; and thereupon the Legislature of each State shall appoint the regimental officers, raise the men, and clothe, arm, and equip them in a soldier-like manner, at the expense of the united States; and the officers and men so clothed, armed, and equipped, shall march to the place appointed, and within the time agreed on by the united States, in congress assembled; but if the united States, in congress assembled, shall, on consideration of circumstances, judge proper that any State should not raise men, or should raise a smaller number than its quota, and that any other State should raise a greater number of men than the quota thereof, such extra number shall be raised, officered, clothed, armed, and equipped in the same manner as the quota of each State, unless the Legislature of such State shall judge that such extra number cannot be safely spared out of the same, in which case they shall raise, officer, clothe, arm, and equip, as many of such extra number as they judge can be safely spared. And the officers and men so clothed, armed, and equipped, shall march to the place appointed, and within the time agreed on by the united States in congress assembled.

The united States, in congress assembled, shall never engage in a war, nor grant letters of marque and reprisal in time of peace, nor enter into any treaties or alliances, nor coin money, nor regulate the value thereof nor ascertain the sums and expenses necessary for the defence and welfare of the united States, or any of them, nor emit bills, nor borrow money on the credit of the united States, nor appropriate money, nor agree upon the number of vessels of war to be built or purchased, or the number of land or sea forces to be raised, nor appoint a commander in chief of the army or navy, unless nine States assent to the same, nor shall a question on any other point, except for adjourning from day to day, be determined, unless by the votes of a majority of the united States in congress assembled.

The congress of the united States shall have power to adjourn to any time within the year, and to any place within the united States, so that no period of adjournment be for a longer duration than the space of six months, and shall publish the journal of their proceedings monthly, except such

parts thereof relating to treaties, alliances, or military operations, as in their judgment require secrecy; and the yeas and
nays of the delegates of each State, on any question, shall be
entered on the journal, when it is desired by any delegate; and
the delegates of a State, or any of them, at his or their request,
shall be furnished with a transcript of the said journal, except
such parts as are above excepted, to lay before the legislatures
of the several States.

ARTICLE X.

The committee of the States, or any nine of them, shall
be authorized to execute, in the recess of congress, such of the
powers of congress as the united States, in congress assembled, by the consent of the nine States, shall, from time to
time, think expedient to vest them with; provided that no
power be delegated to the said committee, for the exercise
of which, by the articles of confederation, the voice of nine
States, in the congress of the united States assembled, be
requisite.

ARTICLE XI.

Canada acceding to this confederation, and joining in
the measures of the united States, shall be admitted into, and
entitled to all the advantages of this union: but no other colony shall be admitted into the same, unless such admission
be agreed to by nine States.

ARTICLE XII.

All bills of credit emitted, monies borrowed, and debts
contracted by or under the authority of congress, before the

assembling of the united States, in pursuance of the present confederation, shall be deemed and considered as a charge against the united States, for payment and satisfaction whereof the said United States, and the public faith are hereby solemnly pleged.

ARTICLE XIII.

Every State shall abide by the determination of the united States, in congress assembled, on all questions which by this confederation are submitted to them. And the articles of this confederation shall be inviolably observed by every State, and the Union shall be perpetual; nor shall any alteration at any time hereafter be made in any of them, unless such alteration be agreed to in a congress of the united States, and be afterwards confirmed by the legislatures of every State.

And Whereas it hath pleased the Great Governor of the World to incline the hearts of the legislatures we respectively represent in congress, to approve of, and to authorize us to ratify the said articles of confederation and perpetual union, Know Ye, that we, the undersigned delegates, by virtue of the power and authority to us given for that purpose, do, by these presents, in the name and in behalf of our respective constituents, fully and entirely ratify and confirm each and every of the said articles of confederation and perpetual union, and all and singular the matters and things therein contained. And we do further solemnly plight and engage the faith of our respective constituents, that they shall abide by the determinations of the united States, in congress assembled, on all questions which by the said confederation are submitted to them; and that the articles thereof shall be inviolably observed by the States we respectively represent, and that the Union shall be perpetual. In witness whereof, we have hereunto set our hands, in Congress. Done at Philadelphia, in the State of Pennsylvania, the ninth day of July, in the year of our Lord one thousand seven hundred and seventy-eight, and in the third year of the Independence of America.

---

www.ourdocuments.gov/doc.php?flash=false&doc=3. Accessed February 19, 2010.

16. The Conditions at Valley Forge

The conditions of the American soldiers were beyond distressing. Here is an example of the difficulties endured (and the spirit in which they were endured) from the pen of Surgeon Albigence Waldo of the Connecticut line, 1777.

December 14.—Prisoners & Deserters are continually coming in. The Army which has been surprisingly healthy hitherto, now begins to grow sickly from the continued fatigues they have suffered this Campaign. Yet they still show a spirit of Alacrity & Contentment not to be expected from so young Troops. I am Sick—discontented—and out of humour. Poor food—hard lodging—Cold Weather—fatigue—Nasty Cloaths—nasty Cookery—Vomit half my time—smoak'd out of my senses—the Devil's in't—I can't Endure it— Why are we sent here to starve and Freeze—What sweet Felicities have I left at home; A charming Wife—pretty

Children—Good Beds—good food—good Cookery—all agreeable—all harmonious. Here all Confusion—smoke & Cold—hunger & filthyness—A pox on my bad luck....

December 16.—Cold Rainy Day, Baggage ordered over the Gulph of our Division, which were to march at Ten, but the baggage was order'd back and for the first time since we have been here the Tents were pitch'd, to keep the men more comfortable. Good morning Brother Soldier (says one to another) how are you? All wet I thank'e, hope you are so (says the other). The Enemy have been at Chestnut Hill Opposite to us near our last encampment the other side Schuylkill, made some Ravages, kill'd two of our Horsemen, taken some prisoners. We have done the like by them....

December 18.—Universal Thanksgiving—a Roasted pig at Night. God be thanked for my health which I have pretty well recovered. How much better should I feel, were I assured my family were in health. But the same good Being who graciously preserves me, is able to preserve them & bring me to the ardently wish'd for enjoyment of them again....

The Army are poorly supplied with Provision, occasioned it is said by the Neglect of the Commissary of Purchases. Much talk among Officers about discharges. Money has become of too little consequence. The Congress have not made their Commissions valuable Enough. Heaven avert the bad consequences of these things!! ...

Our brethren who are unfortunately Prisoners in Philadelphia meet with the most savage and inhumane treatments that Barbarians are Capable of inflicting. Our Enemies do not knock them in the head or burn them with torches to death, or flee them alive, or gradually dismember them till they die, which is customary among Savages & Barbarians. No, they are worse by far. They suffer them to starve, to linger out their lives in extreem hunger. One of these poor unhappy men, drove to the last extreem by the rage of hunger, eat his own fingers up to the first joint from the hand, before he died. Others eat the Clay, the Lime, the Stones of the Prison Walls. Several who died in the Yard had pieces of Bark, Wood, Clay & Stones in their mouths, which the ravings of hunger had caused them to take in for food in the last Agonies of Life! " These are thy *mercies*, O Brittain!"

December 21.—[Valley Forge.] Preparations made for hutts. Provisions Scarce. Mr. Ellis went homeward—sent a Letter to my Wife. Heartily wish myself at home, my Skin & eyes are almost spoil'd with continual smoke. A general cry thro' the Camp this Evening among the Soldiers, "No Meat! No Meat!"—the Distant vales Echo'd back the melancholly sound—"No Meat! No Meat!" Immitating the noise of Crows & Owls, also, made a part of the confused Musick.

What have you for your Dinners Boys? " Nothing but Fire Cake & Water, Sir." At night, " Gentlemen the Supper is ready." What is your Supper Lads? "Fire Cake & Water, Sir." Very poor beef has been drawn in our Camp the greater part of this season. A Butcher bringing a Quarter of this kind of Beef into Camp one day who had white Buttons on the knees of his breeches, a Soldier cries out—"There, there Tom is some more of your fat Beef, by my soul I can see the Butcher's breeches buttons through it." . . .

December 28.—Lay excessive Cold & uncomfortable last Night—my eyes are started out from their Orbits like a Babbit's eyes, occasion'd by a great Cold & Smoke.

The Pennsylvania Magazine of History and Biography, vol. 21 (Philadelphia Historical Society, 1897).

17. LIFE AND DEATH ON A BRITISH PRISON SHIP

Corporal William Slade wrote in his journal of the horrors of the British prison ship Grovnor *during the winter of 1776–1777. He was paroled on January 16, 1777.*

Fort Washington, the 16th day November A. D. 1776. This day I, William Slade, was taken with 2,800 more. We was allowd honours of War. We then marchd to Harlem under guard, where we were turned into a barn. We got little rest that night being very much crowded, (illegible) as some trouble (illegible).

Sunday 17th. Such a Sabbath I never saw. We spent it in sorrow and hunger, haveing no mercy showd.

Monday 18th. We were called out while it was still dark, but was soon marched to New York, four deep, verry much frownd upon by all we saw. We was called Yankey Rebbels a going to the gallows. We got to York at 9 o'clock, were paraded, counted off and marchd to the North Church, where we were confind under guard.

Tuesday 18th. Still confind without provisions till almost night, when we got a little mouldy bisd (biscuit) about four oz. per man. These four days we spent in hunger and sorrow being derided by everry one and calld Rebs.

Wednesday, 20th. We was reinforsd by 300 more. We had 500 before. This causd a Continual Noise and a verry big huddle. Jest at night drawd 6 oz. of Pork per man. This we Eat Alone and Raw.

Thursday, 21st. We passed the Day in sorrow haveing Nothing to Eat or drink but Pamp water . . .

Sunday, 1st. of Decembere 1776. About 300 men was took out and Carried on board the Shipping. Sunday spent in vain.

Munday, 2nd. Early in the morning we was Calld out and stood in the cold, about one hour and then marchd to the North River and went on board The Grovnor transport Ship. There was Now 500 men on board, this made much Confusion. We had to go to bed without supper. This Night was verry Long, hunger Prevaild much. Sorrow more . . .

Friday, 20th. of Decr, 1776. Drawd bisd and butter this morn. Snow and cold. 2 persons Dead on Deck. Last Night verry Long and tiresom. At noon drawd burgo. Prisoners hang their heads and Look Pale. No comfort. All sorrow.

Saturday. 21st. Drawd Bisd. Last Night one of our Regt Got on shore but Got Catched. Troubels come on Comfort gone. At Noon Drawd meat and Rice. Verry cold. Soldiers and Sailors verry Cross. Such melenchoyy times I never saw.

Saturday, 22d. Last Night Nothing but Grones all night of Sick and Dying Men, Amazeing to behold Such hardness, sickness prevails fast. Deaths multiply. Drawd bisd. At noon meat and peas. Weather cold. Sunday gone and No Comfort. Had nothing but sorrow and sadness. All faces sad.

Munday, 23rd. Drawd Bisd and Butter. This morning Sergt Kieth, Job March and several others broke out with the small pox. About 20 Gone from here today that Listed in the king's service. Times Look verry Dark. But we are in hopes of an exchange. One dies almost every Day. Cold but pleasant. Burgo for Dinner. People gone bad with the Pox. . . .

Thursday, 26th. Last Night was spent in Dying Grones and cries. I now gro poorly. Terrible storm as ever I saw. High wind, Drawd bisd. At noon meat and peas. Verry cold and stormy.

Friday, 27th. Three men of our Battalion died Last Night. The most Malencholyest night I ever saw. Small Pox increases fast. This Day I was blooded. Drawd bisd and butter. Stomach all gone. At noon Burgo. Basset is verry sick. Not Like to Live I think.

Thomas Bellows Peck, *William Slade of Windsor, Conn and His Descendants* (Keen, New Hampshire: Sentinal, 1910).

18. "THE BRITISH PRISON SHIP" BY PHILIP MORIN FRENEAU (1781)

In 1780, Freneau was a passenger on the ship Aurora, *traveling from Philadelphia. One day out, the ship was captured by the British. The captain, crew, and passengers were sent to New York as prisoners.*

. . . Two hulks on Hudson's stormy bosom lie,
Two, on the east, alarm the pitying eye—
There, the black SCORPION *at her mooring rides,*
There, STROMBOLO *swings, yielding to the tides;*
Here, bulky JERSEY *fills a larger space,*
And HUNTER, *to all hospitals disgrace—*
    Thou, SCORPION, *fatal to thy crowded throng,*
Dire theme of horror and Plutonian song,
Requir'st my lay—thy sultry decks I know,
And all the torments that exist below!
The briny wave that Hudson's bosom fills
Drain'd through her bottom in a thousand rills:
Rotten and old, replete with sighs and groans,
Scarce on the waters she sustain'd her bones;
Here, doom'd to toil, or founder in the tide,
At the moist pumps incessantly we ply'd,
Here, doom'd to starve, like famish'd dogs, we tore
The scant allowance, that our tyrants bore.
    Remembrance shudders at this scene of fears—
Still in my view some tyrant chief appears,
Some base-born Hessian slave walks threatening by,
Some servile Scot, with murder in his eye,
Still haunts my sight, as vainly they bemoan
Rebellions manag'd so unlike their own!
O may I never feel the poignant pain
To live subjected to such fiends again,
Stewards *and* Mates, *that hostile Britain bore,*
Cut from the gallows on their native shore;
Their ghastly looks and vengeance-beaming eyes

Still to my view in dismal visions rise—
O may I ne'er review these dire abodes,
These piles for slaughter, floating on the floods,—
And you, that o'er the troubled ocean go,
Strike not your standards to this venom'd foe,
Better the greedy wave should swallow all,
Better to meet the death-conducting ball,
Better to sleep on ocean's oozy bed,
At once destroy'd and number'd with the dead,
Than thus to perish in the face of day
Where twice ten thousand deaths one death delay. . . .

Evert A. Duyckinck, ed., *Poem's Relating to the American Revolution*, by Philip Freneau (New York: W.J. Widdleton, 1865).

19. General Washington's Circular Letter to the Governors of Each of the States

In this circular letter to the governors of the states, George Washington bid farewell to the new nation and announced his resignation of his commission. With moving eloquence, he urged the new nation to protect the independence bought with such a high cost. Of particular note is his desire for the Americans to form a strong central government so as to avoid the bickering and squabbling common among the nations of Europe.

Headquarters, Newburgh, New York, June 18, 1783.

Sir—The object for which I had the honor to hold an appointment in the service of my country, being accomplished,

I am now preparing to resign it into the hands of congress, and return to that domestic retirement, which, it is well known, I left with the greatest reluctance; a retirement for which I have never ceased to sigh through a long and painful absence, in which, (remote from the noise and trouble of the world,) I meditate to pass the remainder of life, in a state of undisturbed repose; but, before I carry this resolution into effect, I think it a duty incumbent on me to make this my last official communication, to congratulate you on the glorious events which heaven has been pleased to produce in our favor; to offer my sentiments respecting some important subjects, which appear to me to be intimately connected with the tranquility of the United States; to take my leave of your excellency as a public character; and to give my final blessing to that country, in whose service I have spent the prime of my life; for whose sake I have consumed so many anxious days and watchful nights, and whose happiness, being extremely dear to me, will always constitute no inconsiderable part of my own . . . .

When we consider the magnitude of the prize we contended for, the doubtful nature of the contest and the favorable manner in which it has terminated, we shall find the greatest possible reason for gratitude and rejoicing . . .

The citizens of America, placed in the most enviable condition, as the sole lords and proprietors of a vast tract of continent, comprehending all the various soils and climates of the world, and abounding with all the necessaries and conveniences of life, are now, by the late satisfactory pacification, acknowledged to be possessed of absolute freedom and independency: they are from this period to be considered as the actors on a most conspicuous theatre, which seems to be peculiarly designed by Providence for the display of human greatness and felicity. Here they are not only surrounded with every thing that can contribute to the completion of private and domestic enjoyment, but heaven has crowned all its other blessings, by giving a surer opportunity for political happiness, than any other nation has ever been favored with. . . .

Such is our situation, and such are our prospects. But notwithstanding the cup of blessing is thus reached out to us; notwithstanding happiness is ours, if we have a disposition to seize the occasion, and make it our own, yet it appears to me there is an option still left to the United States of America, whether they will be respectable and prosperous, or contemptible and miserable as a nation. This is the time of their political probation: this is the moment when the eyes of the whole world are turned upon them: this is the time to establish or ruin their national character forever: this is the favorable moment to give such a tone to the federal government, as will enable it to answer the ends of its institution: or, this may be the ill-fated moment for relaxing the powers of the union, annihilating the cement of the confederation, and exposing us to become the sport of European politics, which may play one state against another, to prevent their growing importance, and to serve their own interested purposes. For, according to the system of policy the states shall adopt at this moment, they will stand or fall; and by their confirmation or lapse, it is yet to be decided, whether the revolution must ultimately be considered as a blessing or a curse, not to the present age alone, for with our fate will the destiny of unborn millions be involved . . . .

There are four things which, I humbly conceive, are essential to the well being, I may even venture to say, to the existence, of the United States, as an independent power.

1st. An indissoluble union of the states under one federal head.

2dly. A sacred regard to public justice.

3dly. The adoption of a proper peace establishment. And,

4thly. The prevalence of that pacific and friendly disposition among the people of the United States, which will induce them to forget their local prejudices and policies; to make those mutual concessions which are requisite to the general prosperity; and in some instances, to sacrifice their individual advantages to the interest of the community.

These are the pillars on which the glorious fabric of our independency and national character must be supported. Liberty is the basis—and whoever would dare to sap the foundation, or overturn the structure, under whatever specious pretext he may attempt it, will merit the bitterest execration, and the severest punishment, which can be inflicted by his injured country . . . .

The ability of the country to discharge the debts which have been incurred in its defence, is not to be doubted; and inclination, I flatter myself, will not be wanting. The path of our duty is plain before us; honesty will be found, on every experiment, to be the best and only true policy. Let us then, as a nation, be just; let us fulfil the public contracts which congress had undoubtedly a right to make for the purpose of carrying on the war, with the same good faith we suppose ourselves bound to perform our private engagements. In the meantime, let an attention to the cheerful performance of their proper business, as individuals, and as members of society, be earnestly inculcated on the citizens of America; then will they strengthen the bands of government, and be happy under its protection. Every one will reap the fruit of his labors: every one will enjoy his own acquisitions, without molestation and without danger . . . .

Before I conclude the subject on public justice, I cannot omit to mention the obligations this country is under to that meritorious class of veterans, the non-commissioned officers and privates, who have been discharged for inability, in consequence of the resolution of congress, of the 23d of April, 1782, on an annual pension for life. Their peculiar sufferings, their singular merits and claims to that provision, need only to be known, to interest the feelings of humanity in their behalf. Nothing but a punctual payment of their annual allowance, can rescue them from the most complicated misery; and nothing could be a more melancholy and distressing sight, than to behold those who have shed their blood, or lost their limbs in the service of their country, without a shelter, without a friend, and without the means of obtaining any of the comforts or necessaries of life, compelled to beg their bread daily from door to door. Suffer me to recommend those of this description, belonging to your state, to the warmest patronage of your excellency and your legislature.

It is necessary to say but a few words on the third topic which was proposed, and which regards particularly the defence of the republic—as there can be little doubt but congress will recommend a proper peace establishment for the United States, in which a due attention will be paid to the importance of placing the militia of the union upon a regular and respectable footing. If this should be the case, I should beg leave to urge the great advantage of it in the strongest terms.

The militia of this country must be considered as the palladium of our security, and the first effectual resort in case of hostility. It is essential, therefore, that the same system should pervade the whole; that the formation and discipline of the militia of the continent should be absolutely uniform; and that the same species of arms, accoutrement, and military apparatus, should be introduced in every part of the United States. No one, who has not learned it from experience, can conceive the difficulty, expense, and confusion, which result from a contrary system, or the vague arrangements which have hitherto prevailed. . . .

I have thus freely disclosed what I wished to make known, before I surrendered up my public trust to those who committed it to me. The task is now accomplished; I now bid adieu to your excellency, as the chief magistrate of your state; at the same time I bid a last farewell to the cares of office, and all the employments of public life.

It remains, then, to be my final and only request, that your excellency will communicate these sentiments to your legislature, at their next meeting; and that they may be considered as the legacy of one who has ardently wished, on all occasions, to be useful to his country, and who, even in the shade of retirement, will not fail to implore the Divine benediction upon it.

I now make it my earnest prayer, that God would have you, and the state over which you preside, in his holy protection; that he would incline the hearts of the citizens to cultivate a spirit of subordination and obedience to government; to entertain a brotherly affection and love for one another; for their fellow-citizens of the United States at large, and particularly for their brethren who have served in the field; and, finally, that he would most graciously be pleased to dispose us all to do justice, to love mercy, and to demean ourselves with that charity, humility, and pacific temper of the mind, which were the characteristics of the Divine Author of our blessed religion; without an humble imitation of whose example, in these things, we can never hope to be a happy nation.

I have the honor to be, with much esteem and respect, sir, your excellency's most obedient and most humble servant.

GEORGE WASHINGTON.

Hezekiah Niles, ed., *Centennial Offering: Republication of the Principles and Acts of the Revolution in America* (New York: Barnes & Co., 1876).

IV. FOUNDING

In defeating the British, what had the Americans won? Freedom is the most straightforward answer, but it is also a loaded word, one weighted by responsibilities almost too heavy and numerous to comprehend: operating a peacetime government while paying down wartime debts; establishing relations with foreign governments as a new and independent nation; wrestling with issues such as taxation, political representation, and the growth of bureaucracy; and struggling through questions of basic human rights such as freedom of religion, property rights, *et cetera*, while huge numbers of men and women still lived and died in bondage.

On some fronts, the way was clear, and by the Constitution and Bill of Rights, the people established certain bounds and powers for the new central government. Other issues, such as slavery, took time and blood to decide. The solutions are summarized in some of the amendments to the Constitution, though even those would require the patience, pain, and labors of the people to see bear fruit.

Patience is not one of America's native virtues. But pain and labor are. As Benjamin Franklin's advice for those coming to America shows (item 2 below), Americans are a people who seize opportunity at great personal cost and squeeze from it whatever ounce of improvement they can muster. It is folly to be triumphalist about it. Life in America has always been hard, but as Franklin also intimates, it is unique in the world for being conducive to a happy and fulfilling life.

Freedom is a weight, and freedom is a joy. These founding years of the United States would test and prove it over and again.

1. HECTOR ST. JOHN DE CRÈVECOEUR ASKS, "WHAT IS AN AMERICAN?" (1782)

Hector St. John de Crèvecoeur (1735–1813) was an American author and agriculturist who immigrated from France to North America. After the French and Indian War, he moved to New York, where he became a prosperous farmer. In 1782, in London, he published a collection of essays called Letters from an American Farmer *that described to Europeans the life on the American frontier.*

Here individuals of all nations are melted into a new race of men, whose labours and posterity will one day cause great changes in the world. Americans are the western pilgrims, who are carrying along with them that great mass of arts, sciences, vigour, and industry which began long since in the east; they will finish the great circle. The Americans were once scattered all over Europe; here they are incorporated into one of the finest systems of population which has ever appeared, and which will hereafter become distinct by the power of the different climates they inhabit. The American ought therefore to love this country much better than that wherein either he or his forefathers were born. . . .

The American is a new man, who acts upon new principles; he must therefore entertain new ideas, and form new opinions. From involuntary idleness, servile dependence, penury, and useless labour, he has passed to toils of a very different nature, rewarded by ample subsistence.—This is an American.

Hector St. John de Crèvecoeur, *Letters from an American Farmer* (New York: Fox, Duffield, and Co., 1904).

2. Benjamin Franklin's Advice for Those Coming to America (1784)

In this essay written from his home outside Paris, Franklin explored some of the virtues he believed were necessary for one to be successful in America, such as hard work and self-reliance.

Many persons in Europe having directly or by letters expressed to the writer of this, who is well acquainted with North America, their desire of transporting and establishing themselves in that country; but who appear to him to have formed, through ignorance, mistaken ideas and expectations of what is to be obtained there; he thinks it may be useful, and prevent inconvenient, expensive, and fruitless removals and voyages of improper persons, if he gives some clearer and truer notions of that part of the world than appear to have hitherto prevailed.

He finds it is imagined by numbers, that the inhabitants

of North America are rich, capable of rewarding, and disposed to reward all sorts of ingenuity; that they are at the same time ignorant of all the sciences; and consequently that strangers possessing talents in the belles lettres, fine arts, &c. must be highly esteemed, and so well paid as to become easily rich themselves; that there are also abundance of profitable offices to be disposed of, which the natives are not qualified to fill; and that having few persons of family among them, strangers of birth must be greatly respected, and of course easily obtain the best of those offices which will make all their fortunes: that the governments too, to encourage emigrations from Europe, not only pay the expense of personal transportation, but give lands gratis to strangers with negroes to work for them, utensils of husbandry, and stocks of cattle. These are all wild imaginations; and those who go to America with expectations founded upon them, will surely find themselves disappointed.

The truth is, that though there are in that country few people so miserable as the poor of Europe, there are also very few that in Europe would be called rich: it is rather a general happy mediocrity that prevails. There are few great proprietors of the soil, and few tenants; most people cultivate their own lands, or follow some handicraft or merchandise; very few rich enough to live idly upon their rents or incomes, or to pay the high prices given in Europe for paintings, statues, and the other works of art that are more curious than useful. Hence the natural geniuses that have arisen in America with such talents have universally quitted that country for Europe, where they can be more suitably rewarded. It is true that letters and mathematical knowledge are in esteem there, but they are at the same time more common than is apprehended; there being already existing nine colleges or universities, viz. four in New England, and one in each of the provinces of New York, New Jersey, Pennsylvania, Maryland, and Virginia, all furnished with learned professors; besides a number of smaller academies. These educate many of their youth in the languages and those sciences that qualify men for the professions of divinity, law, or physic. Strangers are indeed by no means excluded from exercising those professions, and the quick increase of inhabitants everywhere gives them chance of employ, which they have in common with the natives. Of civil offices or employments there are few; no superfluous ones as in Europe; and it is a rule established in some of the states, that no office should be so profitable as to make it desirable. The 36th article of the constitution of Pennsylvania runs expressly in these words: "As every freeman, to preserve his independence, (if he has not a sufficient estate) ought to have some profession, calling, trade, or farm, whereby he may honestly subsist, there can be no necessity for, nor use in establishing, offices of profit; the usual effects of which are dependence and servility unbecoming freemen, in the possessors and expectants; faction, contention, corruption, and disorder, among the people. Wherefore, whenever an office, through increase of fees or otherwise, becomes so profitable as to occasion many to apply for it, the profits ought to be lessened by the legislature." These ideas prevailing more or less in all the United States, it cannot be worth any man's while, who has a means of living at home, to expatriate himself in hopes of obtaining a profitable civil office in America; and as to military offices, they are at an end with the war, the armies being disbanded. Much less is it advisable for a person to go thither, who has no other quality to recommend him but his birth. In Europe indeed it has its value, but it is a commodity that cannot be carried to a worse market than to that of America, where people do not inquire concerning a stranger, *What is he?* but, *What can he* DO? If he has any useful art he is welcome, and if he exercises it and behaves well, he will be respected by all that know him; but a mere man of quality, who on that account wants to live upon the public by some office or salary, will be despised and disregarded. The husbandman is in honor there, and even the mechanic, because their employments are useful. The people have a saying, that "God Almighty is himself a mechanic, the greatest in the universe, and he is respected and admired more for the variety, ingenuity, and usefulness of his handyworks, than for the antiquity of his family" . . . According to these opinions of the Americans, one of them would think himself more obliged to a genealogist who could prove for him, that his ancestors and relations for ten generations had been ploughmen, smiths, carpenters, turners, weavers, tanners, or even shoemakers, and consequently that they were useful members of society; than if he could only prove that they were gentlemen, doing nothing of value, but living idly on the labor of others, mere *fruges consumere nati*,* and otherwise *good* for *nothing*, till by their death, their estates . . . come to be *cut up*.

With regard to encouragements for strangers, they

*Editor's Note: Meaning, born merely to consume the fruit of the earth, born merely to eat.

are really only what are derived from good laws and liberty. Strangers are welcome because there is room enough for them all, and therefore the old inhabitants are not jealous of them; the laws protect them sufficiently, so that they have no need of the patronage of great men; and every one will enjoy securely the profits of his industry. But if he does not bring a fortune with him, he must work and be industrious to live. One or two years' residence gives him all the rights of a citizen: but the government does not at present, whatever it may have done in former times, hire people to become settlers, by paying their passages, giving lands, negroes, utensils, stock, or any other kind of emolument whatsoever. In short, America is the land of labor, and by no means what the English call *Lubberland*, and the French *Pays de Cocagne*, where the streets are said to be paved with half-peck loaves, the houses tiled with pancakes, and where the fowls fly about ready roasted, crying, *come eat me!*

Who, then, are the kind of persons to whom an emigration to America may be advantageous? and what are the advantages they may reasonably expect?

Land being cheap in that country, from the vast forests still void of inhabitants, and not likely to be occupied in an age to come, insomuch that the propriety of an hundred acres of fertile soil full of wood may be obtained near the frontiers in many places for eight or ten guineas, hearty young laboring men, who understand husbandry of corn and cattle, which is nearly the same in that country as in Europe, may easily establish themselves there. A little money saved of the good wages they receive there while they work for others, enables them to buy the land and begin their plantation, in which they are assisted by the good-will of their neighbors and some credit. Multitudes of poor people from England, Ireland, Scotland, and Germany, have by this means in a few years become wealthy farmers, who in their own countries, where all the lands are fully occupied, and the wages of labor low, could never have emerged from the mean condition wherein they were born.

From the salubrity of the air, the healthiness of the climate, the plenty of good provisions, and the encouragement to early marriages, by the certainty of subsistence in cultivating the earth, the increase of inhabitants by natural generation is very rapid in America, and becomes more so by the accession of strangers; hence there is a continual demand for more artisans of all the necessary and useful kinds to supply those cultivators of the earth with houses and with furniture, and utensils of the grosser sorts, which cannot so well be brought from Europe. Tolerably good workmen in any of those mechanic arts are sure to find employ, and to be well paid for their work, there being no restraints preventing strangers from exercising any art they understand, nor any permission necessary. If they are poor, they begin first as servants, or journeymen; and if they are sober, industrious, and frugal, they soon become masters, establish themselves in business, marry, raise families, and become respectable citizens.

Lastly, persons of moderate fortunes and capitals, who having a number of children to provide for, are desirous of bringing them up to industry, and to secure estates for their posterity, have opportunities of doing it in America, which

Europe does not afford. There they may be taught and prac-tise profitably mechanic arts, without incurring disgrace on that account; but on the contrary, acquiring respect by such abilities. There small capitals laid out in lands, which daily become more valuable by the increase of people, affords a solid prospect of ample fortunes thereafter for those chil-dren. The writer of this has known several large tracts of land bought on what was then the frontier of Pennsylvania, for ten pounds per hundred acres, which, after 20 years, when the settlement had been extended far beyond them, sold readily, without any improvement made upon them, for three pounds per acre. The acre in America is the same with the English acre or the acre of Normandy.

Those who desire to understand the state of government in America, would do well to read the Constitutions of the several states, and the Articles of Confederation that bind the whole together for general purposes, under the direction of one assembly called the Congress. These Constitutions have been printed by order of Congress in America; two editions of them have also been printed in London, and a good transla-tion of them into French has lately been published at Paris.

Several of the princes of Europe having of late years, from an opinion of advantage to arise by producing all com-modities and manufactures within their own dominions, so as to diminish or render useless their importations, have endeavored to entice workmen from other countries by high salaries, privileges, &c. Many persons pretending to be skilled in various manufactures, imagining that America must be in want of them, and that Congress would probably be disposed to imitate the princes above mentioned, have proposed to go over on condition of having their passages paid, lands given, salaries appointed, exclusive privileges for terms of years, &c. &c. Such persons, on reading the Articles of Confederation, will find that the Congress have no power committed to them, or money put into their hands for such purposes; and that if any such encouragement is given, it must be by the government of some separate state. This however has rarely been done in America; and when it has been done it has rarely succeeded, so as to establish a manufacture which the country was not yet so ripe for as to encourage private persons to set it up, labor being generally too dear there and hands difficult to be kept together, every one desiring to be a master, and the cheapness of lands inclining many to leave trades for agriculture. Some indeed have met with success and are carried on with advantage; but they are generally such as require only a few hands, or wherein great part of the work is performed by machines. Things that are bulky and of so small value as not well to bear the expense of freight, may often be made cheaper in the country than they can be imported; and the manufacture of such things will be profitable wherever there is a sufficient demand. The farmers in America produce indeed a good deal of wool and flax; and none is exported; it is all worked up; but it is in the way of domestic manufacture for the use of the family. The buying up quantities of wool and flax with the design to employ spinners, weavers, &c. and form great establishments, producing quantities of linen and woollen goods for sale, has been several times attempted in different provinces; but those projects have generally failed, goods of equal value being imported cheaper. And when the governments have been solicited to support such schemes by encouragements in money, or by imposing duties on importation of such goods, it has been generally refused, on this principle, that if the country is ripe for the manufacture, it may be carried on by private persons to advantage; and if not, it is a folly to think of forcing nature. Great establishments of manufacture require great numbers of poor to do the work for small wages; these poor are to be found in Europe, but will not be found in America, till the lands are all taken up and cultivated, and the excess of people who cannot get land want employment. The manufacture of silk, they say, is natural in France, as that of cloth in England, because each country produces in plenty the first material: but if England will have a manufacture of silk as well as that of cloth, and France one of cloth as well as that of silk, these unnatural operations must be supported by mutual prohibitions, or higher duties on the importation of each other's goods, by which means the workmen are enabled to tax the home consumer by greater prices, while the higher wages they receive makes them neither happier nor richer, since they only drink more, and work less. Therefore the governments in America do nothing to encourage such projects. The people by this means are not imposed on either by the merchant or mechanic: if the merchant demands too much profit on imported shoes, they buy of the shoemaker; and if he asks too high a price, they take them of the merchant. Thus the two professions are checks on each other. The shoemaker, however, has on the whole a considerable profit upon his labor in America, beyond what he had in Europe, as he can add to his price a sum nearly equal to all the expense of freight and commission, risk or insurance, &c. necessarily charged by the merchant. And the ease is the same with the workmen in every other mechanic art. Hence it is that artisans generally live better and more easily in America than in Europe, and such as are good economists make a comfortable provision for age and for their children: such may therefore remove with advantage to America.

In the old long settled countries of Europe all arts, trades, professions, farms, &c. are so full, that it is difficult for a poor man who has children, to place them where they may gain, or learn to gain a decent livelihood. The artisans who fear creating future rivals in business, refuse to take apprentices, but upon conditions of money, maintenance, and the like, which the parents are unable to comply with. Hence the youth are brought up in ignorance of every gainful art, and obliged to become soldiers, or servants, or thieves, for a subsistence. In America the rapid increase of inhabitants takes away that fear of rivalship, and artisans willingly receive apprentices from the hope of profit by their labor during the remainder of the time stipulated after they shall be instructed. Hence it is easy for poor families to get their children instructed; for the artisans are so desirous of apprentices, that many of them will even give money to the parents to have boys from ten to fifteen years of age bound apprentices to them till the age of twenty-one; and many poor parents have, by that means, on their arrival in the country, raised money enough to buy land sufficient to establish themselves, and to subsist the rest of their family by agriculture. These contracts for apprentices are made before a magistrate, who regulates the agreement according to reason and justice, and having in view the formation of a future useful citizen, obliges the master to engage by a written indenture, not only that during the time of service stipulated the apprentice shall be duly provided with meat, drink, apparel, washing, and lodging, and at its expiration with a complete new suit of clothes, but also that he shall be taught to read, write, and cast accounts, and that he shall be well instructed in the art or profession of his master, or some other, by which he may afterwards gain a livelihood, and be able in his turn to raise a family. A copy of this indenture is given to the apprentice or his friends, and the magistrate keeps a record of it, to which recourse may be had in case of failure by the master in any point of performance. This desire among the masters to have more hands employed in working for them, induces them to pay the passages of young persons, of both sexes, who on their arrival agree to serve them, one, two, three, or four years; those who have already learnt a trade agreeing for a shorter time, in proportion to their skill and the consequent immediate value of their service; and those who have none, agreeing for a longer term, in consideration of being taught an art their poverty would not permit them to acquire in their own country.

The almost general mediocrity of fortune that prevails in America obliging its people to follow some business for subsistence, those vices that arise usually from idleness, are in a great measure prevented. Industry and constant employment are great preservatives of the morals and virtue of a nation. Hence bad examples to youth are more rare in America, which must be a comfortable consideration to parents. To this may be truly added, that serious religion under its various denominations, is not only tolerated, but respected and practised. Atheism is unknown there, infidelity rare and secret, so that persons may live to a great age in that country without having their piety shocked by meeting with either an atheist, or an infidel. And the Divine Being seems to have manifested his approbation of the mutual forbearance and kindness with which the different sects treat each other, by the remarkable prosperity with which he has been pleased to favor the whole country.

Benjamin Franklin, *The Posthumous and Other Writings of Benjamin Franklin*, vol. 1, 2nd ed. (London: Henry Colburn, 1819).

3. FROM "THE HAPPINESS OF AMERICA" BY DAVID HUMPHREYS (1786)

American poet and author David Humphreys (1753–1818) was a 1771 Yale graduate who served as both aide-de-camp and friend to General Washington. His patriotic poems celebrate liberty and democracy and the boundless belief in the possibilities of America and its divine mission.

> *Thrice happy race! how blest were freedom's heirs,*
> *Blest if they knew what happiness is theirs,*
> *Blest if they knew to them alone 't is given*
> *To know no sov'reign but the law and Heaven!*
> *That law for them and Albion's realms alone*

On sacred justice elevates her throne,
Regards the poor, the fatherless protects,
The widow shields, the proud oppressor checks.
Blest if they knew beneath umbrageous trees
To prize the joys of innocence and ease,
Of peace, of health, of temp'rance, toil, and rest,
And the calm sun-shine of the conscious breast.
For them the spring his annual task resumes,
Invests in verdure and adorns in blooms
Earth's parent lap and all her wanton bow'rs
In foliage fair with aromatic flow'rs.
Their fanning wings the zephyrs gently play,
And winnow blossoms from each floating spray;
In bursting buds the embryo fruits appear,
The hope and glory of the rip'ning year.
The mead that courts the scythe, the pastur'd vale,
And garden'd lawn their breathing sweets exhale;
On balmy winds a cloud of fragrance moves,
And floats the odours of a thousand groves;
For them young summer sheds a brighter day,
Matures the germe with his prolific ray,
With prospects cheers, demands more stubborn toil,
And pays their efforts from the grateful soil:
The lofty maize its ears luxurient yields,
The yellow harvests gild the laughing fields,
Extend o'er all th' interminable plain,
And wave in grandeur like the boundless main.
For them the flock o'er green savannas feeds,
For them high-prancing bound the playful steeds,

For them the heifers graze sequester'd dales,
Or pour white nectar in the brimming pails.
To them, what time the hoary frosts draw near,
Ripe autumn brings the labours of the year.
To nature's sons how fair th' autumnal even,
The fading landscape and impurpled heaven,
As from their fields they take their homeward way,
And turn to catch the sun's departing ray! . . .
The cattle fed, the fuel pil'd within,
At setting day the blissful hours begin:
'T is then, sole owner of his little cot,
The farmer feels his independent lot,
Hears with the crackling blaze that lights the wall
The voice of gladness and of nature call,
Beholds his children play, their mother smile,
And tastes with them the fruit of summer's toil.

Walter C. Bronson, ed., *American Poems (1625–1892)* (Chicago: University of Chicago Press, 1912).

4. THOMAS JEFFERSON ON DECENTRALIZED GOVERNMENT AND THE JUDICIARY

In his Autobiography, *Thomas Jefferson remarked on the fact that the judicial branch of government should be independent of the other branches, but not independent of the people. Based on his observation that judges tend to expand their own powers, he felt they should be appointed for limited terms and that their conduct on the bench should affect their reappointments.*

... It is not enough that honest men are appointed Judges. All know the influence of interest on the mind of man, and how unconsciously his judgment is warped by that influence. To this bias add that of the *esprit de corps*, of their peculiar maxim and creed, that "it is the office of a good Judge to enlarge his jurisdiction," and the absence of responsibility; and how can we expect impartial decision between the General government, of which they are themselves so eminent a part, and an individual State, from which they have nothing to hope or fear? We have seen, too, that contrary to all correct example, they are in the habit of going out of the question before them, to throw an anchor ahead, and grapple further hold for future advances of power. They are then, in fact, the corps of sappers and miners, steadily working to undermine the independent rights of the States, and to consolidate all power in the hands of that government in which they have so important a freehold estate. But it is not by the consolidation, or concentration of powers, but by their distribution, that good government is effected. Were not this great country already divided into States, that division must be made, that each might do for itself what concerns itself directly, and what it can so much better do than a distant authority. Every State again is divided into counties, each to take care of what lies within its local bounds; each county again into townships or wards, to manage minuter details; and every ward into farms, to be governed each by its individual proprietor. Were we directed from Washington when to sow, and when to reap, we should soon want bread. It is by this partition of cares, descending in gradation from general to particular, that the mass of human affairs may be best managed, for the good and prosperity of all. I repeat, that I do not charge the Judges with wilful and ill-intentioned error; but honest error must be arrested, where its toleration leads to public ruin. As, for the safety of society, we commit honest maniacs to Bedlam, so judges should be withdrawn from their bench, whose erroneous biases are leading us to dissolution. It may, indeed, injure them in fame or in fortune; but it saves the Republic, which is the first and supreme law.

H. A. Washington, ed., *The Writings of Thomas Jefferson*, vol. 1 (Washington, D.C.: Taylor & Maury, 1853).

5. Benjamin Franklin on the Pursuit of Power and Position

A sobering reminder of what drives many people into government, Franklin's observation, delivered at the Constitutional Convention in 1787, is not so much born of cynicism as it is realism and decades of experience.

Sir, there are two passions which have a powerful influence in the affairs of men. These are ambition and avarice; the love of power and the love of money. Separately, each of these has great force in prompting men to action; but, when united in view of the same object, they have, in many minds, the most violent effects. Place be fore the eyes of such men a post of honor, that shall, at the same time, be a place of profit, and they will move heaven and earth to obtain it. The vast number of such places it is that renders the British Government so tempestuous. The struggles for them are the true source of all those factions which are perpetually dividing the nation, distracting its councils, hurrying it sometimes into fruitless and mischievous wars, and often compelling a submission to dishonorable terms of peace.

And of what kind are the men that will strive for this profitable pre-eminence, through all the bustle of cabal, the heat of contention, the infinite mutual abuse of parties, tearing to pieces the best of characters? It will not be the wise and moderate, the lovers of peace and good order, the men fittest for the trust. It will be the bold and the violent, the men of strong passions and indefatigable activity in their selfish pursuits. These will thrust themselves into your government, and be your rulers. And these, too, will be mistaken in the expected happiness of their situation, for their vanquished competitors, of the same spirit, and from the same motives, will perpetually be endeavoring to distress their administration, thwart their measures, and render them odious to the people.

Mayo Williamson Hazeltine, ed., *Orations from Homer to William McKinley*, vol. 5 (New York: P. F. Collier and Son, 1902).

6. Patrick Henry Calls for an End to Slavery's "Lamentable Evil," January 18, 1773

Many of the founders and other influential leaders of the time had conflicting feelings about the slave trade. For those who were

PATRICK HENRY. Image source: U.S. Library of Congress.
Sketch is from the original painting in the possession of the family.
Etched by Albert Rosenthal, Philadelphia, 1888.

*both slave owners and Christians, it was especially problematic to
defend the practice. Patrick Henry, upon receiving a book from his
friend Robert Pleasants condemning slavery, wrote this letter:*

Dear Sir:—I take this opportunity to acknowledge the
Receipt of Antho Benezet's Book against the Slave trade. I
thank you for it. It is not a little surprising that Christianity,
whose chief Excellence consists in Softening the Human
heart, in cherishing and improving its finer feelings, should
encourage a practice so totally repugnant to the first impressions of Right and Wrong; what adds to the Wonder is, that
this abominable practice has been introduced in the most
enlightened ages. Times that seem to have pretensions to
boast of high Improvements in the arts, sciences, and refined
morality, have brought into general use and guarded by many

Laws, a species of Violence and Tyranny which our most Rude and Barbarous, but more honest Ancestors detested. Is it not amazing that at a time when the Rights of Humanity are defined and understood with precision in a Country above all others fond of Liberty, that in such an age and such a Country we find men professing a Religion the most Humane, mild, meek, gentle and generous, adopting a Principle as repugnant to humanity as it is inconsistent with the Bible and destructive to Liberty ? Every thinking honest man regrets it in specula-tion; how few in practice from Conscientious motives!

The world in general has denied your people a share of its Honours, but the wise will ascribe to you a just Tribute of Virtuous Praise for the Practice of a train of Virtues among which your Disagreement to Slavery will be prin-cipally ranked. I cannot but wish well to a people whose System Imitates the example of Him who was perfect, and believe me I shall honour the Quakers for their noble Effort to abolish Slavery. It is equally calculated to promote moral and political good. Would any one believe I am Master of Slaves of my own Purchase? I am drawn along by the general inconvenience of living without them. I will not, I cannot, justify it. However culpable my conduct I will so far pay my devoir to Virtue as to own the Excellence and rectitude of her Precepts and to lament my want of conformity to them. I believe a time will come when an opportunity will be offered to abolish this lamentable Evil. Everything we can do is to improve it if it happens in Our Day, if not, let us transmit to our Descendants, together with our Slaves, a pity for their unhappy Lot, and an abhorrence for Slavery.

If we cannot reduce this wish'd for Reformation to practice, let us treat the unhappy Victims with lenity; it is the
furtherest advance we can make towards Justice. It is a Debt
we owe to the Purity of our religion, to show that it is at
Variance with that Law which warrants Slavery. Here is an
instance that Silent Meetings, (the Scoff of reverend Doctors),
have done that which learned and Elaborate Preaching could
not effect,—so much preferable are the genuine dictates of
Conscience and Steady attention to its feelings, above the
Teachings of those men who pretend to have found a better
Guide: I exhort you to persevere in so Worthy a Resolution.
Some of your people disagree, or at least are lukewarm in the
abolition of Slavery. Many treat the Resolution of your meeting with Ridicule, and among those who throw contempt on
it are Clergymen whose Surest guard against both Ridicule
and Contempt is a certain act of Assembly. I know not where
to stop, I could say many Things on this subject, a serious
review of which, gives a gloomy perspective to future times.

Excuse this Scrawl, and believe me with Esteem,

YOUR HBLE SER'VT
PATRICK HENRY, JUN'R.

The Friend: A Religious and Literary Journal, vol. 60 (Philadelphia: Wm. H.
Pile's Sons, 1887).

7. THOMAS PAINE ENTREATS AMERICANS TO END SLAVERY, MARCH 8, 1775

*Thomas Paine was one of the earliest and most influential
Americans to denounce the slave trade. His essay "African Slavery*

in America" appeared in the Pennsylvania Journal *and the* Weekly Advertiser *in March of 1775, and the next month he became one of the founding members of the first anti-slavery society in America.*

[T]o go to nations with whom there is no war, who have no way provoked, without farther design of conquest, purely to catch inoffensive people, like wild beasts, for slaves, is an hight of outrage against Humanity and Justice, that seems left by Heathen nations to be practised by pretended Christians. How shameful are all attempts to colour and excuse it!

As these people are not convicted of forfeiting freedom, they have still a natural, perfect right to it; and the Governments whenever they come should, in justice set them free, and punish those who hold them in slavery.

So monstrous is the making and keeping them slaves at all, abstracted from the barbarous usage they suffer, and the many evils attending the practice; as selling husbands away from wives, children from parents, and from each other, in violation of sacred and natural ties ; and opening the way for adulteries, incests, and many shocking consequences, for all of which the guilty Masters must answer to the final Judge.

If the slavery of the parents be unjust, much more is their children's; if the parents were justly slaves, yet the children are born free; this is the natural, perfect right of all mankind; they are nothing but a just recompense to those who bring them up: And as much less is commonly spent on them than others, they have a right, in justice, to be proportionably sooner free.

Certainly one may, with as much reason and decency,

plead for murder, robbery, lewdness, and barbarity, as for this practice: They are not more contrary to the natural dictates of Conscience, and feelings of Humanity; nay, they are all comprehended in it.

But the chief design of this paper is not to disprove it, which many have sufficiently done; but to entreat Americans to consider.

1. With what consistency, or decency they complain so loudly of attempts to enslave them, while they hold so many hundred thousands in slavery; and annually enslave many thousands more, without any pretence of authority, or claim upon them?

2. How just, how suitable to our crime is the punishment with which Providence threatens us? We have enslaved multitudes, and shed much innocent blood in doing it; and now are threatened with the same. And while other evils are confessed, and bewailed, why not this especially, and publicly; than which no other vice, if all others, has brought so much guilt on the land?

3. Whether, then, all ought not immediately to discontinue and renounce it, with grief and abhorrence? Should not every society bear testimony against it, and account obstinate persisters in it bad men, enemies to their country, and exclude them from fellowship; as they often do for much lesser faults ?

4. The great Question may be—What should be done with those who are enslaved already? To turn the old and infirm free, would be injustice and cruelty; they who enjoyed the labours of their better days should keep, and treat them humanely. As to the rest, let prudent men, with the assistance

of legislatures, determine what is practicable for masters, and best for them. Perhaps some could give them lands upon reasonable rent, some, employing them in their labour still, might give them some reasonable allowances for it; so as all may have some property, and fruits of their labours at their own disposal, and be encouraged to industry; the family may live together, and enjoy the natural satisfaction of exercising relative affections and duties, with civil protection, and other advantages, like fellow men. Perhaps they might sometime form useful barrier settlements on the frontiers. Thus they may become interested in the public welfare, and assist in promoting it; instead of being dangerous, as now they are, should any enemy promise them a better condition.

5. The past treatment of Africans must naturally fill them with abhorrence of Christians; lead them to think our religion would make them more inhuman savages, if they embraced it; thus the gain of that trade has been pursued in opposition to the Redeemer's cause, and the happiness of men: Are we not, therefore, bound in duty to him and to them to repair these injuries, as far as possible, by taking some proper measures to instruct, not only the slaves here, but the Africans in their own countries? Primitive Christians laboured always to spread their *Divine Religion*; and this is equally our duty while there is an Heathen nation: But what singular obligations are we under to these injured people!

These are the sentiments of JUSTICE AND HUMANITY.

Moncure Daniel Conway, ed., *The Writings of Thomas Paine*, vol. I (New York & London: Putnam, 1906).

8. George Washington on the
Subject of Slavery

In this April 12, 1786, letter to Robert Morris, George Washington's words reflect his conservative views about the abolition of slavery. As an owner of many slaves, he had a vested interest in the subject. He wrote that he wanted to see slavery abolished by the legislature, but he was also concerned about property loss.

Dear Sir:

I give you the trouble of this letter at the instance of Mr. Dalby of Alexandria, who is called to Philadelphia to attend what he conceives to be a vexatious lawsuit respecting a slave of his, whom a society of Quakers in the city, (formed for such purposes,) have attempted to liberate. The merits of this case will no doubt appear upon trial. From Mr. Dalby's state of the matter, it should seem, that this society is not only acting repugnant to justice, so far as its conduct concerns strangers, but in my opinion impoliticly with respect to the State, the city in particular, without being able, (but by acts of tyranny and oppression,) to accomplish its own ends. He says the conduct of this society is not sanctioned by law. Had the case been otherwise, whatever my opinion of the law might have been, my respect for the policy of the State would on this occasion have appeared in my silence; because against the penalties of promulgated laws one may guard, but there is no avoiding the snares of individuals, or of private societies. If the practice of this society, of which Mr. Dalby speaks, is not discountenanced, none of those, whose *misfortune* it is to have slaves as attendants, will visit the city if they can possibly avoid it; because by so doing they hazard their property, or they must be at the expense (and this will not always succeed) of providing servants of another description.

I hope it will not be conceived from these observations, that it is my wish to hold the unhappy people, who are the subject of this letter, in slavery. I can only say, that there is not a man living, who wishes more sincerely than I do to see a plan adopted for the abolition of it; but there is only one proper and effectual mode by which it can be accomplished, and that is by legislative authority; and this, as far as my suffrage will go, shall never be wanting. But when slaves, who are happy and contented with their present masters, are tampered with and seduced to leave them; when masters are taken unawares by these practices; when a conduct of this sort begets discontent on one side and resentment on the other; and when it happens to fall on a man, whose purse will not measure with that of the society, and he loses his property for want of means to defend it; it is oppression in such a case, and not humanity in any, because it introduces more evils than it can cure.

I will make no apology for writing to you on this subject, for, if Mr. Dalby has not misconceived the matter, an evil exists which requires a remedy; if he has, my intentions have been good, though I may have been too precipitate in this address. Mrs. Washington joins me in every good and kind wish for Mrs. Morris and your family, and I am, &c.

Jared Sparks, ed., *The Writings of George Washington*, vol. 9 (Boston: Ferdinand Andrews, 1839).

9. Selections from *The Federalist Papers*

In October 1787, a series of essays began to appear in two New York newspapers, the Independent Journal *and the* New York Packet. *Titled "The Federalist," the eighty-five essays powerfully advocated the ratification of the United States Constitution. They were all signed "Publius," but the authors were later revealed to be Alexander Hamilton, John Jay, and James Madison. In the years to follow, the essays were compiled into book form, translated into many languages, and became known as* The Federalist Papers. *We have excerpted several passages here below, including all of Madison's Federalist 10, considered one of the most significant of the eighty-five; in it, Madison advocates for an extended republic and writes about the troubles caused by political special interests, or as he calls them, "factions."*

John Jay, Federalist 2, Excerpt

This country and this people seem to have been made for each other, and it appears as if it was the design of Providence, that an inheritance so proper and convenient for a band of brethren, united to each other by the strongest ties, should never be split into a number of unsocial, jealous, and alien sovereignties.

Similar sentiments have hitherto prevailed among all orders and denominations of men among us. To all general purposes we have uniformly been one people; each individual citizen everywhere enjoying the same national rights, privileges, and protection. As a nation we have made peace and war; as a nation we have vanquished our common enemies; as a nation we have formed alliances, and made treaties, and entered into various compacts and conventions with foreign states.

A strong sense of the value and blessings of union induced the people, at a very early period, to institute a federal government to preserve and perpetuate it. They formed it almost as soon as they had a political existence; nay, at a time when their habitations were in flames, when many of their citizens were bleeding, and when the progress of hostility and desolation left little room for those calm and mature inquiries and reflections which must ever precede the formation of a wise and well-balanced government for a free people. It is not to be wondered at, that a government instituted in times so inauspicious, should on experiment be found greatly deficient and inadequate to the purpose it was intended to answer.

This intelligent people perceived and regretted these defects. Still continuing no less attached to union than enamored of liberty, they observed the danger which immediately threatened the former and more remotely the latter; and being pursuaded that ample security for both could only be found in a national government more wisely framed, they, as with one voice, convened the late convention at Philadelphia, to take that important subject under consideration.

This convention, composed of men who possessed the confidence of the people, and many of whom had become highly distinguished by their patriotism, virtue, and wisdom, in times which tried the minds and hearts of men, undertook the arduous task. In the mild season of peace, with minds unoccupied by other subjects, they passed many months in cool, uninterrupted, and daily consultation; and finally, without having been awed by power, or influenced by any passions except love for their country, they presented and recommended to the people the plan produced by their joint and very unanimous councils.

JAMES MADISON, FEDERALIST 10

Among the numerous advantages promised by a well constructed Union, none deserves to be more accurately developed than its tendency to break and control the violence of faction. The friend of popular governments never finds himself so much alarmed for their character and fate, as when he contemplates their propensity to this dangerous vice. He will not fail, therefore, to set a due value on any plan which, without violating the principles to which he is attached, provides a proper cure for it. The instability, injustice, and confusion introduced into the public councils, have, in truth, been the mortal diseases under which popular governments have everywhere perished; as they continue to be the favorite and fruitful topics from which the adversaries to liberty derive their most specious declamations. The valuable improvements made by the American constitutions on the popular models, both ancient and modern, cannot certainly be too much admired; but it would be an unwarrantable partiality, to contend that they have as effectually obviated the danger on this side, as was wished and expected. Complaints are everywhere heard from our most considerate and virtuous citizens, equally the friends of public and private faith, and of public and personal liberty, that our governments are too unstable, that the public good is disregarded in the conflicts of rival parties, and that measures are too often decided, not according to the rules of justice and the rights of the minor party, but by the superior force of an interested and overbearing majority. However anxiously we may wish that these complaints had no foundation, the evidence of known facts will not permit us to deny that they are in some degree true. It will be found, indeed, on a candid review of our situation, that some of the distresses under which we labor have been erroneously charged on the operation of our governments; but it will be found, at the same time, that other causes will not alone account for many of our heaviest misfortunes; and, particularly, for that prevailing and increasing distrust of public engagements, and alarm for private rights, which are echoed from one end of the continent to the other. These must be chiefly, if not wholly, effects of the unsteadiness and injustice with which a factious spirit has tainted our public administrations.

By a faction, I understand a number of citizens, whether amounting to a majority or minority of the whole, who are united and actuated by some common impulse of passion, or of interest, adverse to the rights of other citizens, or to the permanent and aggregate interests of the community.

There are two methods of curing the mischiefs of faction: the one, by removing its causes; the other, by controlling its effects.

There are again two methods of removing the causes of faction: the one, by destroying the liberty which is essential to its existence; the other, by giving to every citizen the same opinions, the same passions, and the same interests.

It could never be more truly said than of the first remedy, that it was worse than the disease. Liberty is to faction what air is to fire, an aliment without which it instantly expires. But it could not be less folly to abolish liberty, which is essential to political life, because it nourishes faction, than it would be to wish the annihilation of air, which is essential to animal life, because it imparts to fire its destructive agency.

The second expedient is as impracticable as the first would be unwise. As long as the reason of man continues fallible, and he is at liberty to exercise it, different opinions will be formed. As long as the connection subsists between his reason and his self-love, his opinions and his passions will have a reciprocal influence on each other; and the former will be objects to which the latter will attach themselves. The diversity in the faculties of men, from which the rights of property originate, is not less an insuperable obstacle to a uniformity of interests. The protection of these faculties is the first object of government. From the protection of different and unequal faculties of acquiring property, the possession of different degrees and kinds of property immediately results; and from the influence of these on the sentiments and views of the respective proprietors, ensues a division of the society into different interests and parties.

The latent causes of faction are thus sown in the nature of man; and we see them everywhere brought into different degrees of activity, according to the different circumstances of civil society. A zeal for different opinions concerning religion, concerning government, and many other points, as well of speculation as of practice; an attachment to different leaders ambitiously contending for pre-eminence and power; or to persons of other descriptions whose fortunes have been interesting to the human passions, have, in turn, divided mankind into parties, inflamed them with mutual animosity, and rendered them much more disposed to vex and oppress each other than to co-operate for their common good. So strong is this propensity of mankind to fall into mutual animosities, that where no substantial occasion presents itself, the most frivolous and fanciful distinctions have been sufficient to kindle their unfriendly passions and excite their most violent conflicts. But the most common and durable source of factions has been the various and unequal distribution of property. Those who hold and those who are without property have ever formed distinct interests in society. Those who are creditors, and those who are debtors, fall under a like discrimination. A landed interest, a manufacturing interest, a mercantile interest, a moneyed interest, with many lesser interests, grow up of necessity in civilized nations, and divide them into different classes, actuated by different sentiments and views. The regulation of these various and interfering interests forms the principal task of modern legislation, and involves the spirit of party and faction in the necessary and ordinary operations of the government.

No man is allowed to be a judge in his own cause, because his interest would certainly bias his judgment, and, not improbably, corrupt his integrity. With equal, nay with greater reason, a body of men are unfit to be both judges and parties at the same time; yet what are many of the most important acts of legislation, but so many judicial determinations, not indeed concerning the rights of single persons, but concerning the rights of large bodies of citizens? And what are the different classes of legislators but advocates and parties to the causes which they determine? Is a law proposed concerning private debts? It is a question to which the creditors are parties on one side and the debtors on the other. Justice ought to hold the balance between them. Yet the parties are, and must be, themselves the judges; and the most numerous party, or, in other words, the most powerful faction must be expected to prevail. Shall domestic manufactures be encouraged, and in what degree, by restrictions on foreign manufactures? are questions which would be differently decided by the landed and the manufacturing classes, and probably by neither with a sole regard to justice and the public good. The apportionment of taxes on the various descriptions of property is an act which seems to require the most exact impartiality; yet there is, perhaps, no legislative act in which greater opportunity and temptation are given to a predominant party to trample on the rules of justice. Every shilling with which they overburden the inferior number, is a shilling saved to their own pockets.

It is in vain to say that enlightened statesmen will be able to adjust these clashing interests, and render them all subservient to the public good. Enlightened statesmen will not always be at the helm. Nor, in many cases, can such an adjustment be made at all without taking into view indirect and remote considerations, which will rarely prevail over the immediate interest which one party may find in disregarding the rights of another or the good of the whole.

The inference to which we are brought is, that the *causes* of faction cannot be removed, and that relief is only to be sought in the means of controlling its *effects*.

If a faction consists of less than a majority, relief is supplied by the republican principle, which enables the majority to defeat its sinister views by regular vote. It may clog the administration, it may convulse the society; but it will be unable to execute and mask its violence under the forms of the Constitution. When a majority is included in a faction, the form of popular government, on the other hand, enables it to sacrifice to its ruling passion or interest both the public good and the rights of other citizens. To secure the public good and private rights against the danger of such a faction, and at the same time to preserve the spirit and the form of popular government, is then the great object to which our inquiries are directed. Let me add that it is the great desideratum by which this form of government can be rescued from the opprobrium under which it has so long labored, and be recommended to the esteem and adoption of mankind.

By what means is this object attainable? Evidently by one of two only. Either the existence of the same passion or interest in a majority at the same time must be prevented, or the majority, having such coexistent passion or interest, must be rendered, by their number and local situation, unable to concert and carry into effect schemes of oppression. If the impulse and the opportunity be suffered to coincide, we well know that neither moral nor religious motives can be relied on as an adequate control. They are not found to be such on the injustice and violence of individuals, and lose their efficacy in proportion to the number combined together, that is, in proportion as their efficacy becomes needful.

From this view of the subject it may be concluded that a pure democracy, by which I mean a society consisting of a small number of citizens, who assemble and administer the government in person, can admit of no cure for the mischiefs of faction.

A common passion or interest will, in almost every case, be felt by a majority of the whole; a communication and concert result from the form of government itself; and there is nothing to check the inducements to sacrifice the weaker party or an obnoxious individual. Hence it is that such democracies have ever been spectacles of turbulence and contention; have ever been found incompatible with personal security or the rights of property ; and have in general been as short in their lives as they have been violent in their deaths. Theoretic politicians, who have patronized this species of government, have erroneously supposed that by reducing mankind to a perfect equality in their political rights, they would, at the same time, be perfectly equalized and assimilated in their possessions, their opinions, and their passions.

A republic, by which I mean a government in which the scheme of representation takes place, opens a different prospect and promises the cure for which we are seeking. Let us examine the points in which it varies from pure democracy, and we shall comprehend both the nature of the cure and the efficacy which it must derive from the Union.

The two great points of difference between a democracy and a republic are: first, the delegation of the government in the latter, to a small number of citizens elected by the rest; secondly, the greater number of citizens, and greater sphere of country, over which the latter may be extended.

The effect of the first difference is, on the one hand, to refine and enlarge the public views, by passing them through the medium of a chosen body of citizens, whose wisdom may best discern the true interest of their country, and whose patriotism and love of justice will be least likely to sacrifice it to temporary or partial considerations. Under such a regulation, it may well happen that the public voice, pronounced by the representatives of the people, will be more consonant to the public good than if pronounced by the people themselves, convened for the purpose. On the other hand, the effect may be inverted. Men of factious tempers, of local prejudices, or of sinister designs, may, *by* intrigue, by corruption, or by other means, first obtain the suffrages, and then betray the interests, of the people. The question resulting is, whether small or extensive republics are more favorable to the election of proper guardians of the public weal; and the latter it is clearly decided in favor of by two obvious considerations :

In the first place, it is to be remarked that however small the republic may be, the representatives must be raised to a certain number, in order to guard against the cabals of a few and that, however large it may be, they must be limited to a certain number, in order to guard against the confusion of a multitude.) Hence, the number of representatives in the two cases not being in proportion to that of the two constituents, and being proportionally greater in the small republic, it follows that, if the proportion of fit characters be not less in the large than in the small republic, the former will present a greater option, and consequently a greater probability of a fit choice.

In the next place, as each representative will be chosen by a greater number of citizens in the large than in the small republic, it will be more difficult for unworthy candidates to practise with success the vicious arts by which elections are too often carried; and the suffrages of the people being more free, will be more likely to centre in men who possess the most attractive merit and the most diffusive and established characters.

It must be confessed that in this, as in most other cases, there is a mean, on both sides of which inconveniences will be found to lie. By enlarging too much the number of electors, you render the representative too little acquainted with all their local circumstances and lesser interests; as by reducing it too much, you render him unduly attached to these, and too little fit to comprehend and pursue great and national objects. The federal Constitution forms a happy combination in this respect; the great and aggregate interests being referred to the national, the local and particular to the State legislatures.

The other point of difference is, the greater number of citizen's and extent of territory which may be brought within the compass of republican than of democratic government; and it is this circumstance principally which renders factious combinations less to be dreaded in the former than in the latter. The smaller the society, the fewer probably will be the distinct parties and interests composing it; the fewer the distinct parties and interests, the more frequently will a majority be found of the same party and the smaller the number of individuals composing a majority, and the smaller the compass within which they are placed, the more easily will they concert and execute their plans of oppression. Extend the sphere, and you take in a greater variety of parties and interests; you make it less probable that a majority of the whole will have a common motive to invade the rights of other citizens; or if such a common motive exists, it will be more difficult for all who feel it to discover their own strength, and to act in unison with each other. Besides other impediments, it may be remarked that, where there is a consciousness of unjust or dishonorable purposes, communication is always checked by distrust in proportion to the number whose concurrence is necessary.

Hence, it clearly appears, that the same advantage which a republic has over a democracy, in controlling the effects of faction, is enjoyed by a large over a small republic,—is enjoyed by the Union over the States composing it. Does the advantage consist in the substitution of representatives whose enlightened views and virtuous sentiments render them superior to local prejudices and to schemes of injustice? It will not be denied that the representation of the Union will be most likely to possess these requisite endowments. Does it consist in the greater security afforded by a greater variety of parties, against the event of any one party being able to outnumber and oppress the rest? In an equal degree does the increased variety of parties comprised within the Union, increase this security. Does it, in fine, consist in the greater obstacles opposed to the concert and accomplishment of the secret wishes of an unjust and interested majority? Here, again, the extent of the Union gives it the most palpable advantage.

The influence of factious leaders may kindle a flame within their particular States, but will be unable to spread a general conflagration through the other States. A religious sect may degenerate into a political faction in a part of the Confederacy; but the variety of sects dispersed over the entire face of it must secure the national councils against any danger from that source. A rage for paper money, for an abolition of debts, for an equal division of property, or for any other improper or wicked project, will be less apt to pervade the whole body of the Union than a particular member of it; in the same proportion as such malady is more likely to taint a particular county or district, than an entire State.

In the extent and proper structure of the Union, therefore, we behold a republican remedy for the diseases most incident to republican government. And according to the degree of pleasure and pride we feel in being republicans, ought to be our zeal in cherishing the spirit and supporting the character of Federalists.

PUBLIUS.

JAMES MADISON, FEDERALIST 42, EXCERPT

It were doubtless to be wished, that the power of prohibiting the importation of slaves had not been postponed until the year 1808, or rather that it had been suffered to have immediate operation. But it is not difficult to account, either for this restriction on the general government, or for the manner in which the whole clause is expressed. It ought to be considered as a great point gained in favor of humanity, that a period of twenty years may terminate forever, within these States, a traffic which has so long and so loudly upbraided the barbarism of modern policy; that within that period, it will receive a considerable discouragement from the federal government, and may be totally abolished, by a concurrence of the few States which continue the unnatural traffic, in the prohibitory example which has been given by so great a majority of the Union. Happy would it be for the unfortunate Africans, if an equal prospect lay before them of being redeemed from the oppressions of their European brethren!

JAMES MADISON, FEDERALIST 43, EXCERPT

"To declare the punishment of treason, but no attainder of treason shall work corruption of blood, or forfeiture, except during the life of the person attainted" [from the U.S. Constitution].

As treason may be committed against the United States, the authority of the United States ought to be enabled to punish it. But as new-fangled and artificial treasons have been the great engines by which violent factions, the natural offspring of free government, have usually wreaked their alternate malignity on each other, the convention have, with great judgment, opposed a barrier to this peculiar danger, by inserting a constitutional definition of the crime, fixing the proof necessary for conviction of it, and restraining the Congress, even in punishing it, from extending the consequences of guilt beyond the person of its author.

ALEXANDER HAMILTON OR JAMES MADISON, FEDERALIST 62, EXCERPT

A good government implies two things: first, fidelity to the object of government, which is the happiness of the people; secondly, a knowledge of the means by which that object can be best attained. Some governments are deficient in both these qualities ; most governments are deficient in the first. I scruple not to assert, that in American governments too little attention has been paid to the last. The federal Constitution avoids this error; and what merits particular notice, it provides for the last in a mode which increases the security for the first . . .

To trace the mischievous effects of a mutable government, would fill a volume. I will hint a few only, each of which will be perceived to be a source of innumerable others.

In the first place, it forfeits the respect and confidence of other nations, and all the advantages connected with national character. An individual who is observed to be inconstant to his plans, or perhaps to carry on his affairs without any plan at all, is marked at once, by all prudent people, as a speedy victim to his own unsteadiness and folly. His more friendly neighbors may pity him, but all will decline to connect their fortunes with his ; and not a few will seize the opportunity of making their fortunes out of his. One nation is to another what one individual is to another; with this melancholy distinction perhaps, that the former, with fewer of the benevolent emotions than the latter, are under fewer restraints also from taking undue advantage from the indiscretions of each other. Every nation, consequently, whose affairs betray a want of wisdom and stability, may calculate on every loss which can be sustained from the more systematic policy of their wiser neighbors. But the best instruction on this subject is unhappily conveyed to America by the example of her own situation. She finds that she is held in no respect by her friends; that she is the derision of her enemies; and that she is a prey to every nation which has an interest in speculating on her fluctuating councils and embarrassed affairs.

The internal effects of a mutable policy are still more calamitous. It poisons the blessing of liberty itself. It will be of little avail to the people, that the laws are made by men of their own choice, if the laws be so voluminous that they cannot be read, or so incoherent that they cannot be understood; if they be repealed or revised before they are promulgated, or undergo such incessant changes that no man, who knows what the law is to-day, can guess what it will be to-morrow. Law is defined to be a rule of action ; but how can that be a rule, which is little known, and less fixed?

Another effect of public instability is the unreasonable advantage it gives to the sagacious, the enterprising, and the moneyed few over the industrious and uninformed mass of the people. Every new regulation concerning commerce or revenue, or in any manner affecting the value of the different species of property, presents a new harvest to those who watch the change, and can trace its consequences; a harvest, reared not by themselves, but by the toils and cares of the great body of their fellow-citizens. This is a state of things in which it may be said with some truth that laws are made for the *few*, not for the *many*.

In another point of view, great injury results from an

unstable government. The want of confidence in the public councils damps every useful undertaking, the success and profit of which may depend on a continuance of existing arrangements. What prudent merchant will hazard his fortunes in any new branch of commerce when he knows not but that his plans may be rendered unlawful before they can be executed ? What farmer or manufacturer will lay himself out for the encouragement given to any particular cultivation or establishment, when he can have no assurance that his preparatory labors and advances will not render him a victim to an inconstant government ? In a word, no great improvement or laudable enterprise can go forward which requires the auspices of a steady system of national policy.

But the most deplorable effect of all is that diminution of attachment and reverence which steals into the hearts of the people, towards a political system which betrays so many marks of infirmity, and disappoints so many of their flattering hopes. No government, any more than an individual, will long be respected without being truly respectable; nor be truly respectable, without possessing a certain portion of order and stability.

Henry Cabot Lodge, ed., *The Federalist: A Commentary on the Constitution of the United States* (New York: G.P. Putnam's Sons, 1888).

10. THE CONSTITUTION OF THE UNITED STATES

After the Revolutionary War ended in 1783, the states faced new problems. In peacetime there were new issues that the Articles of

Confederation didn't adequately address: paying a large public war debt, enforcing law and order, regulating trade, dealing with Indian tribes, and negotiating with other governments. In May of 1787, the Federal Convention convened in Philadelphia, where the delegates decided that rather than revising the Articles of Confederation, they would create a new and stronger Constitution. The debate lasted all summer as the founding fathers crafted a system of government that would define the rights and liberties of the American people and provide for three branches of government, none of which would have dominance over the others. The Constitution was first ratified on December 7, 1787, by Delaware and went into effect on June 11, 1788, when New Hampshire ratified it. It has since been amended twenty-seven times, including the Bill of Rights. This is the original version of the Constitution; we've italicized portions that were later amended or suspended.

WE THE PEOPLE of the United States, in Order to form a more perfect Union, establish Justice, insure domestic Tranquility, provide for the common defence, promote the general Welfare, and secure the Blessings of Liberty to ourselves and our Posterity, do ordain and establish this Constitution for the United States of America.

ARTICLE. I.

SECTION. 1.

All legislative Powers herein granted shall be vested in a Congress of the United States, which shall consist of a Senate and House of Representatives.

SECTION. 2.

The House of Representatives shall be composed of Members chosen every second Year by the People of the several States, and the Electors in each State shall have the Qualifications requisite for Electors of the most numerous Branch of the State Legislature.

No Person shall be a Representative who shall not have attained to the Age of twenty five Years, and been seven Years a Citizen of the United States, and who shall not, when elected, be an Inhabitant of that State in which he shall be chosen.

Representatives and direct Taxes shall be apportioned among the several States which may be included within this Union, according to their respective Numbers, which shall be determined by adding to the whole Number of free Persons, including those bound to Service for a Term of Years, and excluding Indians not taxed, three fifths of all other Persons. The actual Enumeration shall be made within three Years after the first Meeting of the Congress of the United States, and within every subsequent Term of ten Years, in such Manner as they shall by Law direct. The Number of Representatives shall not exceed one for every thirty Thousand, but each State shall have at Least one Representative; and until such enumeration shall be made, the State of New Hampshire shall be entitled to chuse three, Massachusetts eight, Rhode-Island and Providence Plantations one, Connecticut five, New-York six, New Jersey four, Pennsylvania eight, Delaware one, Maryland six, Virginia ten, North Carolina five, South Carolina five, and Georgia three.

When vacancies happen in the Representation from any State, the Executive Authority thereof shall issue Writs of Election to fill such Vacancies.

The House of Representatives shall chuse their Speaker and other Officers; and shall have the sole Power of Impeachment.

SECTION. 3.

The Senate of the United States shall be composed of two Senators from each State, *chosen by the Legislature* thereof for six Years; and each Senator shall have one Vote.

Immediately after they shall be assembled in Consequence of the first Election, they shall be divided as equally as may be into three Classes. The Seats of the Senators of the first Class shall be vacated at the Expiration of the second Year, of the second Class at the Expiration of the fourth Year, and of the third Class at the Expiration of the sixth Year, so that one third may be chosen every second Year; *and if Vacancies happen by Resignation, or otherwise, during the Recess of the Legislature of any State, the Executive thereof may make temporary Appointments until the next Meeting of the Legislature, which shall then fill such Vacancies.*

No Person shall be a Senator who shall not have attained to the Age of thirty Years, and been nine Years a Citizen of the United States, and who shall not, when elected, be an Inhabitant of that State for which he shall be chosen.

The Vice President of the United States shall be President of the Senate, but shall have no Vote, unless they be equally divided.

The Senate shall chuse their other Officers, and also a President pro tempore, in the Absence of the Vice President, or when he shall exercise the Office of President of the United States.

The Senate shall have the sole Power to try all Impeachments. When sitting for that Purpose, they shall be on Oath or Affirmation. When the President of the United States is tried, the Chief Justice shall preside: And no Person shall be convicted without the Concurrence of two thirds of the Members present.

Judgment in Cases of Impeachment shall not extend further than to removal from Office, and disqualification to hold and enjoy any Office of honor, Trust or Profit under the United States: but the Party convicted shall nevertheless be liable and subject to Indictment, Trial, Judgment and Punishment, according to Law.

SECTION. 4.

The Times, Places and Manner of holding Elections for Senators and Representatives, shall be prescribed in each State by the Legislature thereof; but the Congress may at any time by Law make or alter such Regulations, except as to the Places of chusing Senators.

The Congress shall assemble at least once in every Year, and such Meeting shall *be on the first Monday in December*, unless they shall by Law appoint a different Day.

SECTION. 5.

Each House shall be the Judge of the Elections, Returns

and Qualifications of its own Members, and a Majority of each shall constitute a Quorum to do Business; but a smaller Number may adjourn from day to day, and may be authorized to compel the Attendance of absent Members, in such Manner, and under such Penalties as each House may provide.

Each House may determine the Rules of its Proceedings, punish its Members for disorderly Behaviour, and, with the Concurrence of two thirds, expel a Member.

Each House shall keep a Journal of its Proceedings, and from time to time publish the same, excepting such Parts as may in their Judgment require Secrecy; and the Yeas and Nays of the Members of either House on any question shall, at the Desire of one fifth of those Present, be entered on the Journal.

Neither House, during the Session of Congress, shall, without the Consent of the other, adjourn for more than three days, nor to any other Place than that in which the two Houses shall be sitting.

Section. 6.

The Senators and Representatives shall receive a Compensation for their Services, to be ascertained by Law, and paid out of the Treasury of the United States. They shall in all Cases, except Treason, Felony and Breach of the Peace, be privileged from Arrest during their Attendance at the Session of their respective Houses, and in going to and returning from the same; and for any Speech or Debate in either House, they shall not be questioned in any other Place.

No Senator or Representative shall, during the Time for which he was elected, be appointed to any civil Office under the Authority of the United States, which shall have been created, or the Emoluments whereof shall have been encreased during such time; and no Person holding any Office under the United States, shall be a Member of either House during his Continuance in Office.

SECTION. 7.

All Bills for raising Revenue shall originate in the House of Representatives; but the Senate may propose or concur with Amendments as on other Bills.

Every Bill which shall have passed the House of Representatives and the Senate, shall, before it become a Law, be presented to the President of the United States: If he approve he shall sign it, but if not he shall return it, with his Objections to that House in which it shall have originated, who shall enter the Objections at large on their Journal, and proceed to reconsider it. If after such Reconsideration two thirds of that House shall agree to pass the Bill, it shall be sent, together with the Objections, to the other House, by which it shall likewise be reconsidered, and if approved by two thirds of that House, it shall become a Law. But in all such Cases the Votes of both Houses shall be determined by yeas and Nays, and the Names of the Persons voting for and against the Bill shall be entered on the Journal of each House respectively. If any Bill shall not be returned by the President within ten Days (Sundays excepted) after it shall have been presented to him, the Same shall be a Law, in like Manner as if he had signed it, unless the Congress by their Adjournment prevent its Return, in which Case it shall not be a Law.

Every Order, Resolution, or Vote to which the Concurrence of the Senate and House of Representatives may be necessary (except on a question of Adjournment) shall be presented to the President of the United States; and before the Same shall take Effect, shall be approved by him, or being disapproved by him, shall be repassed by two thirds of the Senate and House of Representatives, according to the Rules and Limitations prescribed in the Case of a Bill.

Section. 8.

The Congress shall have Power To lay and collect Taxes, Duties, Imposts and Excises, to pay the Debts and provide for the common Defence and general Welfare of the United States; but all Duties, Imposts and Excises shall be uniform throughout the United States;

To borrow Money on the credit of the United States;

To regulate Commerce with foreign Nations, and among the several States, and with the Indian Tribes;

To establish an uniform Rule of Naturalization, and uniform Laws on the subject of Bankruptcies throughout the United States;

To coin Money, regulate the Value thereof, and of foreign Coin, and fix the Standard of Weights and Measures;

To provide for the Punishment of counterfeiting the Securities and current Coin of the United States;

To establish Post Offices and post Roads;

To promote the Progress of Science and useful Arts,

by securing for limited Times to Authors and Inventors the exclusive Right to their respective Writings and Discoveries;

To constitute Tribunals inferior to the supreme Court;

To define and punish Piracies and Felonies committed on the high Seas, and Offences against the Law of Nations;

To declare War, grant Letters of Marque and Reprisal, and make Rules concerning Captures on Land and Water;

To raise and support Armies, but no Appropriation of Money to that Use shall be for a longer Term than two Years;

To provide and maintain a Navy;

To make Rules for the Government and Regulation of the land and naval Forces;

To provide for calling forth the Militia to execute the Laws of the Union, suppress Insurrections and repel Invasions;

To provide for organizing, arming, and disciplining, the Militia, and for governing such Part of them as may be employed in the Service of the United States, reserving to the States respectively, the Appointment of the Officers, and the Authority of training the Militia according to the discipline prescribed by Congress;

To exercise exclusive Legislation in all Cases whatsoever, over such District (not exceeding ten Miles square) as may, by Cession of particular States, and the Acceptance of Congress, become the Seat of the Government of the United States, and to exercise like Authority over all Places purchased by the Consent of the Legislature of the State in which the Same shall be, for the Erection of Forts, Magazines, Arsenals, dock-Yards, and other needful Buildings;—And

To make all Laws which shall be necessary and proper for carrying into Execution the foregoing Powers, and all other Powers vested by this Constitution in the Government of the United States, or in any Department or Officer thereof.

SECTION. 9.

The Migration or Importation of such Persons as any of the States now existing shall think proper to admit, shall not be prohibited by the Congress prior to the Year one thousand eight hundred and eight, but a Tax or duty may be imposed on such Importation, not exceeding ten dollars for each Person.

The Privilege of the Writ of Habeas Corpus shall not be suspended, unless when in Cases of Rebellion or Invasion the public Safety may require it.

No Bill of Attainder or ex post facto Law shall be passed.

No Capitation, or other direct, Tax shall be laid, *unless in Proportion to the Census or enumeration herein before directed to be taken.*

No Tax or Duty shall be laid on Articles exported from any State.

No Preference shall be given by any Regulation of Commerce or Revenue to the Ports of one State over those of another; nor shall Vessels bound to, or from, one State, be obliged to enter, clear, or pay Duties in another.

No Money shall be drawn from the Treasury, but in Consequence of Appropriations made by Law; and a regular Statement and Account of the Receipts and Expenditures of all public Money shall be published from time to time.

No Title of Nobility shall be granted by the United States: And no Person holding any Office of Profit or Trust under them, shall, without the Consent of the Congress, accept of any present, Emolument, Office, or Title, of any kind whatever, from any King, Prince, or foreign State.

Section. 10.

No State shall enter into any Treaty, Alliance, or Confederation; grant Letters of Marque and Reprisal; coin Money; emit Bills of Credit; make any Thing but gold and silver Coin a Tender in Payment of Debts; pass any Bill of Attainder, ex post facto Law, or Law impairing the Obligation of Contracts, or grant any Title of Nobility.

No State shall, without the Consent of the Congress, lay any Imposts or Duties on Imports or Exports, except what may be absolutely necessary for executing it's inspection Laws: and the net Produce of all Duties and Imposts, laid by any State on Imports or Exports, shall be for the Use of the Treasury of the United States; and all such Laws shall be subject to the Revision and Controul of the Congress.

No State shall, without the Consent of Congress, lay any Duty of Tonnage, keep Troops, or Ships of War in time of Peace, enter into any Agreement or Compact with another State, or with a foreign Power, or engage in War, unless actually invaded, or in such imminent Danger as will not admit of delay.

Article. II.

Section. 1.

The executive Power shall be vested in a President of the

United States of America. He shall hold his Office during the Term of four Years, and, together with the Vice President, chosen for the same Term, be elected, as follows:

Each State shall appoint, in such Manner as the Legislature thereof may direct, a Number of Electors, equal to the whole Number of Senators and Representatives to which the State may be entitled in the Congress: but no Senator or Representative, or Person holding an Office of Trust or Profit under the United States, shall be appointed an Elector.

The Electors shall meet in their respective States, and vote by Ballot for two Persons, of whom one at least shall not be an Inhabitant of the same State with themselves. And they shall make a List of all the Persons voted for, and of the Number of Votes for each; which List they shall sign and certify, and transmit sealed to the Seat of the Government of the United States, directed to the President of the Senate. The President of the Senate shall, in the Presence of the Senate and House of Representatives, open all the Certificates, and the Votes shall then be counted. The Person having the greatest Number of Votes shall be the President, if such Number be a Majority of the whole Number of Electors appointed; and if there be more than one who have such Majority, and have an equal Number of Votes, then the House of Representatives shall immediately chuse by Ballot one of them for President; and if no Person have a Majority, then from the five highest on the List the said House shall in like Manner chuse the President. But in chusing the President, the Votes shall be taken by States, the Representation from each State having one Vote; A quorum for this purpose shall consist of a Member or Members from two thirds of the States, and a Majority of all the States shall be necessary to a Choice. In every Case, after the Choice of the President, the Person having the greatest Number of Votes of the Electors shall be the Vice President. But if there should remain two or more who have equal Votes, the Senate shall chuse from them by Ballot the Vice President.

The Congress may determine the Time of chusing the Electors, and the Day on which they shall give their Votes; which Day shall be the same throughout the United States.

No Person except a natural born Citizen, or a Citizen of the United States, at the time of the Adoption of this Constitution, shall be eligible to the Office of President; neither shall any Person be eligible to that Office who shall not have attained to the Age of thirty five Years, and been fourteen Years a Resident within the United States.

In Case of the Removal of the President from Office, or of his Death, Resignation, or Inability to discharge the Powers and Duties of the said Office, the Same shall devolve on the Vice President, and the Congress may by Law provide for the Case of Removal, Death, Resignation or Inability, both of the President and Vice President, declaring what Officer shall then act as President, and such Officer shall act accordingly, until the Disability be removed, or a President shall be elected.

The President shall, at stated Times, receive for his Services, a Compensation, which shall neither be increased nor diminished during the Period for which he shall have been elected, and he shall not receive within that Period any other Emolument from the United States, or any of them.

Before he enter on the Execution of his Office, he shall take the following Oath or Affirmation:—"I do solemnly swear (or affirm) that I will faithfully execute the Office of President of the United States, and will to the best of my Ability, preserve, protect and defend the Constitution of the United States."

SECTION. 2.

The President shall be Commander in Chief of the Army and Navy of the United States, and of the Militia of the several States, when called into the actual Service of the United States; he may require the Opinion, in writing, of the principal Officer in each of the executive Departments, upon any Subject relating to the Duties of their respective Offices, and he shall have Power to grant Reprieves and Pardons for Offences against the United States, except in Cases of Impeachment.

He shall have Power, by and with the Advice and Consent of the Senate, to make Treaties, provided two thirds of the Senators present concur; and he shall nominate, and by and with the Advice and Consent of the Senate, shall appoint Ambassadors, other public Ministers and Consuls, Judges of the supreme Court, and all other Officers of the United States, whose Appointments are not herein otherwise provided for, and which shall be established by Law: but the Congress may by Law vest the Appointment of such inferior Officers, as they think proper, in the President alone, in the Courts of Law, or in the Heads of Departments.

The President shall have Power to fill up all Vacancies that may happen during the Recess of the Senate, by granting

Commissions which shall expire at the End of their next Session.

Section. 3.

He shall from time to time give to the Congress Information of the State of the Union, and recommend to their Consideration such Measures as he shall judge necessary and expedient; he may, on extraordinary Occasions, convene both Houses, or either of them, and in Case of Disagreement between them, with Respect to the Time of Adjournment, he may adjourn them to such Time as he shall think proper; he shall receive Ambassadors and other public Ministers; he shall take Care that the Laws be faithfully executed, and shall Commission all the Officers of the United States.

Section. 4.

The President, Vice President and all civil Officers of the United States, shall be removed from Office on Impeachment for, and Conviction of, Treason, Bribery, or other high Crimes and Misdemeanors.

Article. III.

Section. 1.

The judicial Power of the United States shall be vested in one supreme Court, and in such inferior Courts as the Congress may from time to time ordain and establish. The Judges, both of the supreme and inferior Courts, shall hold their Offices during good Behaviour, and shall, at stated Times, receive for their Services a Compensation, which shall not be diminished during their Continuance in Office.

SECTION. 2.

The judicial Power shall extend to all Cases, in Law and Equity, arising under this Constitution, the Laws of the United States, and Treaties made, or which shall be made, under their Authority;—to all Cases affecting Ambassadors, other public Ministers and Consuls;—to all Cases of admiralty and maritime Jurisdiction;—to Controversies to which the United States shall be a Party;—to Controversies between two or more States;—*between a State and Citizens of another State*,—between Citizens of different States,—between Citizens of the same State claiming Lands under Grants of different States, and between a State, or the Citizens thereof, and foreign States, Citizens or Subjects.

In all Cases affecting Ambassadors, other public Ministers and Consuls, and those in which a State shall be Party, the supreme Court shall have original Jurisdiction. In all the other Cases before mentioned, the supreme Court shall have appellate Jurisdiction, both as to Law and Fact, with such Exceptions, and under such Regulations as the Congress shall make.

The Trial of all Crimes, except in Cases of Impeachment, shall be by Jury; and such Trial shall be held in the State where the said Crimes shall have been committed; but when not committed within any State, the Trial shall be at such Place or Places as the Congress may by Law have directed.

Section. 3.

Treason against the United States, shall consist only in levying War against them, or in adhering to their Enemies, giving them Aid and Comfort. No Person shall be convicted of Treason unless on the Testimony of two Witnesses to the same overt Act, or on Confession in open Court.

The Congress shall have Power to declare the Punishment of Treason, but no Attainder of Treason shall work Corruption of Blood, or Forfeiture except during the Life of the Person attainted.

Article. IV.

Section. 1.

Full Faith and Credit shall be given in each State to the public Acts, Records, and judicial Proceedings of every other State. And the Congress may by general Laws prescribe the Manner in which such Acts, Records and Proceedings shall be proved, and the Effect thereof.

Section. 2.

The Citizens of each State shall be entitled to all Privileges and Immunities of Citizens in the several States.

A Person charged in any State with Treason, Felony, or other Crime, who shall flee from Justice, and be found in another State, shall on Demand of the executive Authority of the State from which he fled, be delivered up, to be removed to the State having Jurisdiction of the Crime.

No Person held to Service or Labour in one State, under the Laws thereof, escaping into another, shall, in Consequence of any Law or Regulation therein, be discharged from such Service or Labour, but shall be delivered up on Claim of the Party to whom such Service or Labour may be due.

Section. 3.

New States may be admitted by the Congress into this Union; but no new State shall be formed or erected within the Jurisdiction of any other State; nor any State be formed by the Junction of two or more States, or Parts of States, without the Consent of the Legislatures of the States concerned as well as of the Congress.

The Congress shall have Power to dispose of and make all needful Rules and Regulations respecting the Territory or other Property belonging to the United States; and nothing in this Constitution shall be so construed as to Prejudice any Claims of the United States, or of any particular State.

Section. 4.

The United States shall guarantee to every State in this Union a Republican Form of Government, and shall protect each of them against Invasion; and on Application of the Legislature, or of the Executive (when the Legislature cannot be convened), against domestic Violence.

Article. V.

The Congress, whenever two thirds of both Houses shall deem it necessary, shall propose Amendments to this Constitution, or, on the Application of the Legislatures of two thirds of the several States, shall call a Convention for proposing Amendments, which, in either Case, shall be valid to all Intents and Purposes, as Part of this Constitution, when ratified by the Legislatures of three fourths of the several States, or by Conventions in three fourths thereof, as the one or the other Mode of Ratification may be proposed by the Congress; Provided that no Amendment which may be made prior to the Year One thousand eight hundred and eight shall in any Manner affect the first and fourth Clauses in the Ninth Section of the first Article; and that no State, without its Consent, shall be deprived of its equal Suffrage in the Senate.

Article. VI.

All Debts contracted and Engagements entered into, before the Adoption of this Constitution, shall be as valid against the United States under this Constitution, as under the Confederation.

This Constitution, and the Laws of the United States which shall be made in Pursuance thereof; and all Treaties made, or which shall be made, under the Authority of the United States, shall be the supreme Law of the Land; and the Judges in every State shall be bound thereby, any Thing in the Constitution or Laws of any State to the Contrary notwithstanding.

The Senators and Representatives before mentioned, and the Members of the several State Legislatures, and all executive and judicial Officers, both of the United States and of the several States, shall be bound by Oath or Affirmation, to support this Constitution; but no religious Test shall ever be required as a Qualification to any Office or public Trust under the United States.

Article. VII.

The Ratification of the Conventions of nine States, shall be sufficient for the Establishment of this Constitution between the States so ratifying the Same.

The Word, "the," being interlined between the seventh and eighth Lines of the first Page, the Word "Thirty" being partly written on an Erazure in the fifteenth Line of the first Page, The Words "is tried" being interlined between the thirty second and thirty third Lines of the first Page and the Word "the" being interlined between the forty third and forty fourth Lines of the second Page.

Attest William Jackson Secretary

Done in Convention by the Unanimous Consent of the States present the Seventeenth Day of September in the Year of our Lord one thousand seven hundred and Eighty seven and of the Independence of the United States of America the Twelfth In witness whereof We have hereunto subscribed our Names,

Gº. Washington
Presidt and deputy from Virginia

Delaware

Geo: Read   Jaco: Broom

Gunning Bedford jun

John Dickinson

Richard Bassett

Maryland
James McHenry
Dan of St Thos. Jenifer
Danl. Carroll

Virginia
John Blair
James Madison Jr.

North Carolina
Wm. Blount
Richd. Dobbs Spaight
Hu Williamson

South Carolina
J. Rutledge
Charles Cotesworth
    Pinckney
Charles Pinckney
Pierce Butler

Georgia
William Few
Abr Baldwin

New Hampshire
John Langdon
Nicholas Gilman

Massachusetts
Nathaniel Gorham
Rufus King

Connecticut
Wm. Saml. Johnson
Roger Sherman

New York
Alexander Hamilton

New Jersey
Wil: Livingston
David Brearley
Wm. Paterson
Jona: Dayton

Pennsylvania
B Franklin
Thomas Mifflin
Robt. Morris
Geo. Clymer
Thos. FitzSimons
Jared Ingersoll
James Wilson
Gouv Morris

www.archives.gov/exhibits/charters/constitution.html. Accessed December 21, 2009.

11. Jack Nips on Constitution, Bill of Rights, and Freedom of Religion

Baptist minister John Leland (1754–1841) helped lead the fight to ratify the Constitution in Massachusetts. He wrote "The Yankee Spy" (under the pseudonym of Jack Nips) to champion the separation of church and state.

Question. Why are men obliged, every year, to pay their taxes?

Answer. To support government.

Q. What is government?

A. The government here intended, is the mutual compact of a certain body of people, for the general safety of their lives, liberty, and property.

Q. Are all systems of civil government founded in compact?

A. No: successful robbers and tyrants have founded their systems in *conquest*—enthusiasts and priest-ridden people have founded theirs in *grace*—while men without merit have founded their system in *birth*; but the true principle, that all Gentile nations should found their government upon, is, *compact*. . . .

Q. What have you to say about the Federal Constitution of America?

A. It is a novelty in the world: partly confederate, and partly consolidate—partly directly elective, and partly elective one or two removes from the people;

but one of the great excellencies of the Constitution is, that no religious test is ever to be required to qualify any officer in any part of the government. To say that the Constitution is perfect, would be too high an encomium upon the fallibility of the framers of it; yet this may be said, that it is the best national machine that is now in existence. . . .

Q. What is your opinion of having a *bill of rights* to a constitution of government?

A. Whenever it is understood that all power is in the monarch—that subjects possess nothing of their own, but receive all from the potentate, then the liberty of the people is commensurate with the bill of rights that is squeezed out of the monarch.

After the conquest of William, the government of England was completely monarchical, until the reign of king John, when the Magna Charta was given to the people: this has often been mentioned in America as a sufficient reason for a *bill of rights*, to preface each constitution: but in republican, representative governments, like those of America, where it is understood that all power is originally in the *people*, and that all is still retained in their hands, except so much as for a limited time is given to the rulers, where is the propriety of having a bill of rights? In this view, no such bill is found in the Federal Constitution.

But it is not my intention, at this time, to dispute the point of propriety or impropriety of a bill of rights, but shall only add that the liberty of the people depends more upon the organization of government, the responsibility of rulers, and the faithful discharge of the officers, than it does upon any bill of rights that can be named. . . .

If the constitution should be revised, and anything about religion should be said in it, the following paragraph is proposed:—

"To prevent the evils that have heretofore been occasioned in the world by religious establishments, and to keep up the proper distinction between religion and politics, no religious test shall ever be requested as a qualification of any officer, in any department of this government; neither shall the legislature, under this constitution, ever establish any religion by law, give any one sect a preference to another, or force any man in the commonwealth to part with his property for the support of religious worship, or the maintenance of ministers of the gospel."

John Leland and L. F. Greene, *The Writings of the Late Elder John Leland* (New York: G. W. Wood, 1845).

12. JOEL BARLOW ON SEPARATION OF CHURCH AND STATE

American writer and diplomat Joel Barlow (1754–1812) wrote an open letter (a brief selection of which is included below) in 1791 to the National Convention of France, analyzing the

French Constitution from the view of American principles. His letter won him French citizenship, which was undoubtedly a pleasant perk, though not his primary motivation.

I know it is asserted and believed by some well-wishers to society, that religion would be lost among men, if they were to banish all legal establishments with regard to the manner of exercising it. I should not be so perfectly convinced as I am of the absurdity of this opinion, were it not easy to discover how it came to be introduced. It is an idea, as I believe, purely political; and it had its origin in the supposed necessity of governing men by fraud,—of erecting their credulity into an hierarchy, in order to sustain the despotism of the state. I hold religion to be a natural propensity of the mind, as respiration is of the lungs. If this be true, there can be no danger of its being lost: and I can see no more reason for making laws to regulate the impression of Deity upon the soul, than there would be, to regulate the action of light upon the eye, or of air upon the lungs.

Charles S. Hyneman and Donald S. Lutz, eds., *American Political Writing During the Founding Era*, vol. 2, (Indianapolis: Liberty Fund, 1983).

13. THE BILL OF RIGHTS

By 1789 the United States Constitution had already been ratified, but many of the founding fathers—with fresh memories of the British violations of their human and civil rights—were wary of the potential tyranny of a strong central government. They demanded a "bill of rights" to protect the rights of the citizens. On December 15, 1791, the first ten amendments to the Constitution, known as the Bill of Rights, were ratified. Amendments 11 through 27 were proposed and ratified at various times thereafter, the most curious of all being Amendment 27, which was proposed in 1789 and not ratified until more than two hundred years later in 1992. Though these later amendments fall well outside the chronological bounds of this project, we have included them all here, as we did not want to follow the example of so many political practitioners and leave out the parts that failed to fit our scheme.

THE PREAMBLE TO THE BILL OF RIGHTS

Congress of the United States begun and held at the City of New-York, on Wednesday the fourth of March, one thousand seven hundred and eighty nine.

THE Conventions of a number of the States, having at the time of their adopting the Constitution, expressed a desire, in order to prevent misconstruction or abuse of its powers, that further declaratory and restrictive clauses should be added: And as extending the ground of public confidence in the Government, will best ensure the beneficent ends of its institution.

RESOLVED by the Senate and House of Representatives of the United States of America, in Congress assembled, two thirds of both Houses concurring, that the following Articles be proposed to the Legislatures of the several States, as amendments to the Constitution of the United States, all, or any of which Articles, when ratified by three fourths of the said Legislatures, to be valid to all intents and purposes, as part of the said Constitution; viz.

ARTICLES in addition to, and Amendment of the Constitution of the United States of America, proposed by Congress, and ratified by the Legislatures of the several States, pursuant to the fifth Article of the original Constitution.

Amendment I

Congress shall make no law respecting an establishment of religion, or prohibiting the free exercise thereof; or abridging the freedom of speech, or of the press; or the right of the people peaceably to assemble, and to petition the Government for a redress of grievances.

Amendment II

A well regulated Militia, being necessary to the security of a free State, the right of the people to keep and bear Arms, shall not be infringed.

Amendment III

No Soldier shall, in time of peace be quartered in any house, without the consent of the Owner, nor in time of war, but in a manner to be prescribed by law.

Amendment IV

The right of the people to be secure in their persons, houses, papers, and effects, against unreasonable searches and seizures, shall not be violated, and no Warrants shall issue, but upon probable cause, supported by Oath or affirmation, and particularly describing the place to be searched, and the persons or things to be seized.

AMENDMENT V

No person shall be held to answer for a capital, or otherwise infamous crime, unless on a presentment or indictment of a Grand Jury, except in cases arising in the land or naval forces, or in the Militia, when in actual service in time of War or public danger; nor shall any person be subject for the same offence to be twice put in jeopardy of life or limb; nor shall be compelled in any criminal case to be a witness against himself, nor be deprived of life, liberty, or property, without due process of law; nor shall private property be taken for public use, without just compensation.

AMENDMENT VI

In all criminal prosecutions, the accused shall enjoy the right to a speedy and public trial, by an impartial jury of the State and district wherein the crime shall have been committed, which district shall have been previously ascertained by law, and to be informed of the nature and cause of the accusation; to be confronted with the witnesses against him; to have compulsory process for obtaining witnesses in his favor, and to have the Assistance of Counsel for his defence.

AMENDMENT VII

In Suits at common law, where the value in controversy shall exceed twenty dollars, the right of trial by jury shall be preserved, and no fact tried by a jury, shall be otherwise re-examined in any Court of the United States, than according to the rules of the common law.

AMENDMENT VIII

Excessive bail shall not be required, nor excessive fines imposed, nor cruel and unusual punishments inflicted.

AMENDMENT IX

The enumeration in the Constitution, of certain rights, shall not be construed to deny or disparage others retained by the people.

AMENDMENT X

The powers not delegated to the United States by the Constitution, nor prohibited by it to the States, are reserved to the States respectively, or to the people.

---

www.archives.gov/exhibits/charters/bill_of_rights.html. Accessed December 21, 2009.

14. AMENDMENTS XI THROUGH XXVII

It is a testament to the founding fathers that the United States Constitution has only been amended twenty-seven times since it was ratified over two hundred years ago, and ten of those comprised the Bill of Rights. Amendments XI through XXVII were ratified between 1795 and 1992.

AMENDMENT XI

[*Passed by Congress March 4, 1794. Ratified February 7,*

1795. Article III, section 2, of the Constitution was modified by
amendment 11.]

The Judicial power of the United States shall not be
construed to extend to any suit in law or equity, commenced
or prosecuted against one of the United States by Citizens
of another State, or by Citizens or Subjects of any Foreign
State.

AMENDMENT XII

[*Passed by Congress December 9, 1803. Ratified June 15,
1804. A portion of Article II, section 1 of the Constitution was
superseded by the 12th amendment.*]

The Electors shall meet in their respective states and vote
by ballot for President and Vice-President, one of whom, at
least, shall not be an inhabitant of the same state with themselves; they shall name in their ballots the person voted for
as President, and in distinct ballots the person voted for as
Vice-President, and they shall make distinct lists of all persons voted for as President, and of all persons voted for as
Vice-President, and of the number of votes for each, which
lists they shall sign and certify, and transmit sealed to the
seat of the government of the United States, directed to the
President of the Senate;—the President of the Senate shall,
in the presence of the Senate and House of Representatives,
open all the certificates and the votes shall then be counted;—
The person having the greatest number of votes for President,
shall be the President, if such number be a majority of the
whole number of Electors appointed; and if no person have
such majority, then from the persons having the highest

numbers not exceeding three on the list of those voted for as President, the House of Representatives shall choose immediately, by ballot, the President. But in choosing the President, the votes shall be taken by states, the representation from each state having one vote; a quorum for this purpose shall consist of a member or members from two-thirds of the states, and a majority of all the states shall be necessary to a choice. [And if the House of Representatives shall not choose a President whenever the right of choice shall devolve upon them, before the fourth day of March next following, then the Vice-President shall act as President, as in case of the death or other constitutional disability of the President.—]* The person having the greatest number of votes as Vice-President, shall be the Vice-President, if such number be a majority of the whole number of Electors appointed, and if no person have a majority, then from the two highest numbers on the list, the Senate shall choose the Vice-President; a quorum for the purpose shall consist of two-thirds of the whole number of Senators, and a majority of the whole number shall be necessary to a choice. But no person constitutionally ineligible to the office of President shall be eligible to that of Vice-President of the United States.

*Superseded by section 3 of the 20th amendment.

AMENDMENT XIII
[Passed by Congress January 31, 1865. Ratified December 6, 1865. A portion of Article IV, section 2, of the Constitution was superseded by the 13th amendment.]

SECTION 1.

Neither slavery nor involuntary servitude, except as a punishment for crime whereof the party shall have been duly convicted, shall exist within the United States, or any place subject to their jurisdiction.

SECTION 2.

Congress shall have power to enforce this article by appropriate legislation.

AMENDMENT XIV

[Passed by Congress June 13, 1866. Ratified July 9, 1868. Article I, section 2, of the Constitution was modified by section 2 of the 14th amendment.]

SECTION 1.

All persons born or naturalized in the United States, and subject to the jurisdiction thereof, are citizens of the United States and of the State wherein they reside. No State shall make or enforce any law which shall abridge the privileges or immunities of citizens of the United States; nor shall any State deprive any person of life, liberty, or property, without due process of law; nor deny to any person within its jurisdiction the equal protection of the laws.

SECTION 2.

Representatives shall be apportioned among the several States according to their respective numbers, counting the whole number of persons in each State, excluding Indians not taxed. But when the right to vote at any election for the choice of electors for President and Vice-President of the United States, Representatives in Congress, the Executive and Judicial officers of a State, or the members of the Legislature thereof, is denied to any of the male inhabitants of such State, being twenty-one years of age,* and citizens of the United States, or in any way abridged, except for participation in rebellion, or other crime, the basis of representation therein shall be reduced in the proportion which the number of such male citizens shall bear to the whole number of male citizens twenty-one years of age in such State.

Changed by section 1 of the 26th amendment.

Section 3.

No person shall be a Senator or Representative in Congress, or elector of President and Vice-President, or hold any office, civil or military, under the United States, or under any State, who, having previously taken an oath, as a member of Congress, or as an officer of the United States, or as a member of any State legislature, or as an executive or judicial officer of any State, to support the Constitution of the United States, shall have engaged in insurrection or rebellion against the same, or given aid or comfort to the enemies thereof. But Congress may by a vote of two-thirds of each House, remove such disability.

Section 4.

The validity of the public debt of the United States, authorized by law, including debts incurred for payment of pensions and bounties for services in suppressing insurrection or rebellion, shall not be questioned. But neither the United States nor any State shall assume or pay any debt or obligation incurred in aid of insurrection or rebellion against the United States, or any claim for the loss or emancipation of any slave; but all such debts, obligations and claims shall be held illegal and void.

SECTION 5.

The Congress shall have the power to enforce, by appropriate legislation, the provisions of this article.

AMENDMENT XV

[Passed by Congress February 26, 1869. Ratified February 3, 1870.]

SECTION 1.

The right of citizens of the United States to vote shall not be denied or abridged by the United States or by any State on account of race, color, or previous condition of servitude—

SECTION 2.

The Congress shall have the power to enforce this article by appropriate legislation.

AMENDMENT XVI

[Passed by Congress July 2, 1909. Ratified February 3, 1913. Article I, section 9, of the Constitution was modified by amendment 16.]

The Congress shall have power to lay and collect taxes on incomes, from whatever source derived, without apportionment among the several States, and without regard to any census or enumeration.

AMENDMENT XVII

[Passed by Congress May 13, 1912. Ratified April 8, 1913. Article I, section 3, of the Constitution was modified by the 17th amendment.]

The Senate of the United States shall be composed of two Senators from each State, elected by the people thereof, for six years; and each Senator shall have one vote. The electors in each State shall have the qualifications requisite for electors of the most numerous branch of the State legislatures.

When vacancies happen in the representation of any State in the Senate, the executive authority of such State shall issue writs of election to fill such vacancies: *Provided*, That the legislature of any State may empower the executive thereof to make temporary appointments until the people fill the vacancies by election as the legislature may direct.

This amendment shall not be so construed as to affect the election or term of any Senator chosen before it becomes valid as part of the Constitution.

AMENDMENT XVIII

[Passed by Congress December 18, 1917. Ratified January 16, 1919. Repealed by amendment 21.]

SECTION 1.

After one year from the ratification of this article the

manufacture, sale, or transportation of intoxicating liquors within, the importation thereof into, or the exportation thereof from the United States and all territory subject to the jurisdiction thereof for beverage purposes is hereby prohibited.

Section 2.

The Congress and the several States shall have concurrent power to enforce this article by appropriate legislation.

Section 3.

This article shall be inoperative unless it shall have been ratified as an amendment to the Constitution by the legislatures of the several States, as provided in the Constitution, within seven years from the date of the submission hereof to the States by the Congress.

Amendment XIX

[Passed by Congress June 4, 1919. Ratified August 18, 1920.]

The right of citizens of the United States to vote shall not be denied or abridged by the United States or by any State on account of sex.

Congress shall have power to enforce this article by appropriate legislation.

Amendment XX

[Passed by Congress March 2, 1932. Ratified January 23, 1933. Article I, section 4, of the Constitution was modified by section 2 of this amendment. In addition, a portion of the 12th amendment was superseded by section 3.]

SECTION 1.

The terms of the President and the Vice President shall end at noon on the 20th day of January, and the terms of Senators and Representatives at noon on the 3d day of January, of the years in which such terms would have ended if this article had not been ratified; and the terms of their successors shall then begin.

SECTION 2.

The Congress shall assemble at least once in every year, and such meeting shall begin at noon on the 3d day of January, unless they shall by law appoint a different day.

SECTION 3.

If, at the time fixed for the beginning of the term of the President, the President elect shall have died, the Vice President elect shall become President. If a President shall not have been chosen before the time fixed for the beginning of his term, or if the President elect shall have failed to qualify, then the Vice President elect shall act as President until a President shall have qualified; and the Congress may by law provide for the case wherein neither a President elect nor a Vice President shall have qualified, declaring who shall then act as President, or the manner in which one who is to act shall be selected, and such person shall act accordingly until a President or Vice President shall have qualified.

SECTION 4.

The Congress may by law provide for the case of the death of any of the persons from whom the House of

Representatives may choose a President whenever the right of choice shall have devolved upon them, and for the case of the death of any of the persons from whom the Senate may choose a Vice President whenever the right of choice shall have devolved upon them.

Section 5.

Sections 1 and 2 shall take effect on the 15th day of October following the ratification of this article.

Section 6.

This article shall be inoperative unless it shall have been ratified as an amendment to the Constitution by the legislatures of three-fourths of the several States within seven years from the date of its submission.

Amendment XXI

[*Passed by Congress February 20, 1933. Ratified December 5, 1933.*]

Section 1.

The eighteenth article of amendment to the Constitution of the United States is hereby repealed.

Section 2.

The transportation or importation into any State, Territory, or Possession of the United States for delivery or use therein of intoxicating liquors, in violation of the laws thereof, is hereby prohibited.

SECTION 3.

This article shall be inoperative unless it shall have been ratified as an amendment to the Constitution by conventions in the several States, as provided in the Constitution, within seven years from the date of the submission hereof to the States by the Congress.

AMENDMENT XXII

[*Passed by Congress March 21, 1947. Ratified February 27, 1951.*]

SECTION 1.

No person shall be elected to the office of the President more than twice, and no person who has held the office of President, or acted as President, for more than two years of a term to which some other person was elected President shall be elected to the office of President more than once. But this Article shall not apply to any person holding the office of President when this Article was proposed by Congress, and shall not prevent any person who may be holding the office of President, or acting as President, during the term within which this Article becomes operative from holding the office of President or acting as President during the remainder of such term.

SECTION 2.

This article shall be inoperative unless it shall have been ratified as an amendment to the Constitution by the legislatures of three-fourths of the several States within seven years from the date of its submission to the States by the Congress.

Amendment XXIII

[*Passed by Congress June 16, 1960. Ratified March 29, 1961.*]

Section 1.

The District constituting the seat of Government of the United States shall appoint in such manner as Congress may direct:

A number of electors of President and Vice President equal to the whole number of Senators and Representatives in Congress to which the District would be entitled if it were a State, but in no event more than the least populous State; they shall be in addition to those appointed by the States, but they shall be considered, for the purposes of the election of President and Vice President, to be electors appointed by a State; and they shall meet in the District and perform such duties as provided by the twelfth article of amendment.

Section 2.

The Congress shall have power to enforce this article by appropriate legislation.

Amendment XXIV

[*Passed by Congress August 27, 1962. Ratified January 23, 1964.*]

Section 1.

The right of citizens of the United States to vote in any primary or other election for President or Vice President, for electors for President or Vice President, or for Senator or

Representative in Congress, shall not be denied or abridged by the United States or any State by reason of failure to pay poll tax or other tax.

Section 2.

The Congress shall have power to enforce this article by appropriate legislation.

Amendment XXV

[*Passed by Congress July 6, 1965. Ratified February 10, 1967. Article II, section 1, of the Constitution was affected by the 25th amendment.*]

Section 1.

In case of the removal of the President from office or of his death or resignation, the Vice President shall become President.

Section 2.

Whenever there is a vacancy in the office of the Vice President, the President shall nominate a Vice President who shall take office upon confirmation by a majority vote of both Houses of Congress.

Section 3.

Whenever the President transmits to the President pro tempore of the Senate and the Speaker of the House of Representatives his written declaration that he is unable to discharge the powers and duties of his office, and until he transmits to them a written declaration to the contrary, such powers and duties shall be discharged by the Vice President as Acting President.

SECTION 4.

Whenever the Vice President and a majority of either the principal officers of the executive departments or of such other body as Congress may by law provide, transmit to the President pro tempore of the Senate and the Speaker of the House of Representatives their written declaration that the President is unable to discharge the powers and duties of his office, the Vice President shall immediately assume the powers and duties of the office as Acting President.

Thereafter, when the President transmits to the President pro tempore of the Senate and the Speaker of the House of Representatives his written declaration that no inability exists, he shall resume the powers and duties of his office unless the Vice President and a majority of either the principal officers of the executive department or of such other body as Congress may by law provide, transmit within four days to the President pro tempore of the Senate and the Speaker of the House of Representatives their written declaration that the President is unable to discharge the powers and duties of his office. Thereupon Congress shall decide the issue, assembling within forty-eight hours for that purpose if not in session. If the Congress, within twenty-one days after receipt of the latter written declaration, or, if Congress is not in session, within twenty-one days after Congress is required to assemble, determines by two-thirds vote of both Houses that the President is unable to discharge the powers and duties of his office, the Vice President shall continue to discharge the same as Acting President; otherwise, the President shall resume the powers and duties of his office.

Amendment XXVI

[Passed by Congress March 23, 1971. Ratified July 1, 1971. Amendment 14, section 2, of the Constitution was modified by section 1 of the 26th amendment.]

Section 1.

The right of citizens of the United States, who are eighteen years of age or older, to vote shall not be denied or abridged by the United States or by any State on account of age.

Section 2.

The Congress shall have power to enforce this article by appropriate legislation.

Amendment XXVII

[Originally proposed Sept. 25, 1789. Ratified May 7, 1992.]

No law, varying the compensation for the services of the Senators and Representatives, shall take effect, until an election of representatives shall have intervened.

---

www.archives.gov/exhibits/charters/constitution_amendments_11-27.html. Accessed December 21, 2009.

Thomas Paine holding a copy of his book, *Rights of Man*.
Image source: U.S. Library of Congress. Artist George Romney.

15. Thomas Paine on Despotism through Bureaucracies (1791)

Paine here drills into one of the great difficulties with large and powerful governments of any sort—the army of bureaucrats (which means, basically, "government by men who sit at desks") who enforce the myriad laws and statutes. If democracy and republican government are essentially about efficient rule, protecting the rights of citizens, and allowing redress when they've been wronged, then bureaucracy is fundamentally at odds with democratic and republican government. It's a story that goes back to the complaints by the earliest settlers about the king's customs men who enforced the Navigation Acts, and it continues through to this very day.

When despotism has established itself for ages in a country, as in France, it is not in the person of the King only that it resides. It has the appearance of being so in show, and in nominal authority; but it is not so in practice, and in fact. It has its standard every where. Every office and department has its despotism founded upon custom and usage. Every place has its Bastille, and every Bastille its despot. The original hereditary despotism, resident in the person of the King, divides and subdivides itself into a thousand shapes and forms, till at last the whole of it is acted by deputation. This was the case in France; and against this species of despotism, proceeding on through an endless labyrinth of office till the source of it is scarcely perceptible, there is no mode of redress. It strengthens itself by assuming the appearance of duty, and tyrannizes under the pretense of obeying.

Thomas Payne, *Rights of Man* (London: J.S. Jordan, 1791).

16. THOMAS PAINE ON UNEQUAL TAXATION

The founders, like Paine, generally believed that the laws should apply equally to all citizens. And given the sore spot of taxes, unequal taxation was a particularly important issue.

Excess and inequality of taxation, however disguised in the means, never fail to appear in their effects. As a great mass of the community are thrown thereby into poverty and discontent, they are constantly on the brink of commotion; and deprived, as they unfortunately are, of the means of information, are easily heated to outrage. Whatever the apparent cause of any riots may be, the real one is always want of happiness. It shows that something is wrong in the system of Government that injures the felicity by which society is to be preserved.

Thomas Payne, *Rights of Man* (London: Watts & Co., 1906).

17. TIMOTHY STONE'S 1792 ELECTION SERMON

Timothy Stone was a Congregationalist minister from Connecticut. In this 1792 sermon he was speaking to the governor and legislature of that state regarding—among other things, such as the need for true community—the importance of righteousness of those in authority.

But when party spirit, local views, and interested motives, direct their suffrages, when they lose sight of the great end of government the public good, and give themselves up, to the baneful influence of parasitical demagogues, they may well expect to reap the bitter fruits of their own folly, in a partial wavering administration. Through the neglect, or abuse of their privileges, most states have lost their liberties; and have fallen a prey to the avarice and ambition of designing and wicked men. "When the righteous are in authority, the people rejoice: but when the wicked beareth rule, the people mourn." This joy, or mourning, among a people, greatly depends on their own conduct in elections—bribery here, is the bane of society—the man who will give or receive a reward in this case, must be extremely ignorant, not to deserve the stigma of an enemy to the state—and should he have address to avoid discovery, he must be destitute of sensibility, not to feel himself to be despicable. All private dishonorable methods to raise persons to office, convey a strong suspicion to the discerning mind, that merit is wanting: real merit may dwell in obscurity, but it needeth not, neither will it ever solicit, the aids of corruption to bring itself into view. When streams are polluted in their fountain they will not fail to run impure— offices in government obtained by purchase, will always be improved to regain the purchase money with large increase: and a venal administration will possess neither disposition nor strength to correct the vices of others, but will lose sight of the public happiness, in the eager pursuit of personal emolument. . . .

Religion and civil government, are not one and the same thing: tho' both may, and are designed to embrace some of the same objects, yet the former, extends its obligations and designs immensely beyond what the latter can pretend to: and it hath rights and prerogatives, with which the latter may not intermeddle. Still, there are many ways, in which civil government may give countenance, encouragement, and even support to religion, without invading the prerogatives of the Most High; or, touching the inferior, tho sacred rights of conscience: and in doing of which, it may not only shew its friendly regard to christianity, but derive important advantages to itself.

Charles S. Hyneman and Donald S. Lutz, eds., *American Political Writing During the Founding Era*, vol. 2 (Indianapolis: Liberty Fund, 1983).

18. Joseph Hopkinson's "Hail, Columbia!" (1798)

It wasn't until 1931 that "The Star-Spangled Banner" was officially adopted as America's national anthem. Before that, the song "Hail, Columbia!" served in that capacity for many events. Lawyer and congressman Joseph Hopkinson (1770–1842) penned the lyrics for it, and Philip Phile wrote the melody. They wrote it for the inauguration of George Washington, and today it is played when the vice president enters an event (as "Hail to the Chief" is for the president).

> Hail, Columbia! happy land!
> Hail, ye heroes, heav'n born band!
> > Who fought and bled in Freedom's cause,
> > Who fought and bled in Freedom's cause,
> And when the storm of war was gone,
> Enjoyed the peace your valor won.
> > Let independence be our boast,
> > Ever mindful what it cost,
> Ever grateful for the prize,
> Let its altar reach the skies.

CHORUS:
> Firm, united, let us be,
> Rallying round our liberty!
> As a band of brothers joined,
> Peace and safety we shall find.

Immortal patriots, rise once more!
Defend your rights, defend your shore!
> Let no rude foe, with impious hand,
> Let no rude foe, with impious hand,

Invade the shrine where sacred lies,
Of toil and blood the well-earned prize.
> While off'ring peace sincere and just,
> In heaven we place a manly trust,

That truth and justice shall prevail,
And every scheme of bondage fail.

Nicholas Smith, *Stories of Great National Songs* (Milwaukee: Young Churchman, 1899).

V. Republic

—————

The early days of America were full of promise and troubles. Along with the opening of the western frontier and the growth of a national economy came a contentious clash of political parties, another war with Britain, and economic embargos and their associated travail.

The wisdom of men like Washington and Jefferson (while not always compatible) helped keep America on balance in these years, though others such as Noah Webster were already seeing and warning about potential flaws in the American system that would curtail freedom and lead to a loss of liberty. Webster's message: Don't lose sight of what our forebears endured and gained. Let their example embolden and empower us to hold fast to that which was won.

1. The First Inaugural Address of George Washington

Delivered to a joint session of Congress, Washington here speaks of "the sacred fire of liberty," "the propitious smiles of Heaven," and "the experiment entrusted to the hands of the American people."

Fellow Citizens of the Senate and the House of Representatives.
Among the vicissitudes incident to life, no event could have filled me with greater anxieties than that of which the

notification was transmitted by your order, and received on the fourteenth day of the present month. On the one hand, I was summoned by my Country, whose voice I can never hear but with veneration and love, from a retreat which I had chosen with the fondest predilection, and, in my flattering hopes, with an immutable decision, as the asylum of my declining years: a retreat which was rendered every day more necessary as well as more dear to me, by the addition of habit to inclination, and of frequent interruptions in my health to the gradual waste committed on it by time. On the other hand, the magnitude and difficulty of the trust to which the voice of my Country called me, being sufficient to awaken in the wisest and most experienced of her citizens, a distrustful scrutiny into his qualifications, could not but overwhelm with dispondence, one, who, inheriting inferior endowments from nature and unpractised in the duties of civil administration, ought to be peculiarly conscious of his own deficiencies. In this conflict of emotions, all I dare aver, is, that it has been my faithful study to collect my duty from a just appreciation of every circumstance, by which it might be affected. All I dare hope, is, that, if in executing this task I have been too much swayed by a grateful remembrance of former instances, or by an affectionate sensibility to this transcendent proof, of the confidence of my fellow-citizens; and have thence too little consulted my incapacity as well as disinclination for the weighty and untried cares before me; my error will be palliated by the motives which misled me, and its consequences be judged by my Country, with some share of the partiality in which they originated.

Such being the impressions under which I have, in

obedience to the public summons, repaired to the present station; it would be peculiarly improper to omit in this first official Act, my fervent supplications to that Almighty Being who rules over the Universe, who presides in the Councils of Nations, and whose providential aids can supply every human defect, that his benediction may consecrate to the liberties and happiness of the People of the United States, a Government instituted by themselves for these essential purposes: and may enable every instrument employed in its administration to execute with success, the functions allotted to his charge. In tendering this homage to the Great Author of every public and private good I assure myself that it expresses your sentiments not less than my own; nor those of my fellow-citizens at large, less than either. No People can be bound to acknowledge and adore the invisible hand, which conducts the Affairs of men more than the People of the United States. Every step, by which they have advanced to the character of an independent nation, seems to have been distinguished by some token of providential agency. And in the important revolution just accomplished in the system of their United Government, the tranquil deliberations and voluntary consent of so many distinct communities, from which the event has resulted, cannot be compared with the means by which most Governments have been established, without some return of pious gratitude along with an humble anticipation of the future blessings which the past seem to presage. These reflections, arising out of the present crisis, have forced themselves too strongly on my mind to be suppressed. You will join with me I trust in thinking, that there are none under the influence of which, the proceedings of a new and free Government can more auspiciously commence.

By the article establishing the Executive Department, it is made the duty of the President "to recommend to your consideration, such measures as he shall judge necessary and expedient." The circumstances under which I now meet you, will acquit me from entering into that subject, farther than to refer to the Great Constitutional Charter under which you are assembled; and which, in defining your powers, designates the objects to which your attention is to be given. It will be more consistent with those circumstances, and far more congenial with the feelings which actuate me, to substitute, in place of a recommendation of particular measures, the tribute that is due to the talents, the rectitude, and the patriotism which adorn the characters selected to devise and adopt them. In these honorable qualifications, I behold the surest pledges, that as on one side, no local prejudices, or attachments; no seperate views, nor party animosities, will misdirect the comprehensive and equal eye which ought to watch over this great assemblage of communities and interests: so, on another, that the foundations of our National policy will be laid in the pure and immutable principles of private morality; and the preeminence of a free Government, be exemplified by all the attributes which can win the affections of its Citizens, and command the respect of the world.

I dwell on this prospect with every satisfaction which an ardent love for my Country can inspire: since there is no truth more thoroughly established, than that there exists in the oeconomy and course of nature, an indissoluble union between virtue and happiness, between duty and advantage, between the genuine maxims of an honest and magnanimous policy, and the solid rewards of public prosperity and felicity: Since we ought to be no less persuaded that the propitious smiles of Heaven, can never be expected on a nation that disregards the eternal rules of order and right, which Heaven itself has ordained: And since the preservation of the sacred fire of liberty, and the destiny of the Republican model of Government, are justly considered as deeply, perhaps as finally staked, on the experiment entrusted to the hands of the American people.

Besides the ordinary objects submitted to your care, it will remain with your judgment to decide, how far an exercise of the occasional power delegated by the Fifth article of the Constitution is rendered expedient at the present juncture by the nature of objections which have been urged against the System, or by the degree of inquietude which has given birth to them. Instead of undertaking particular recommendations on this subject, in which I could be guided by no lights derived from official opportunities, I shall again give way to my entire confidence in your discernment and pursuit of the public good: For I assure myself that whilst you carefully avoid every alteration which might endanger the benefits of an United and effective Government, or which ought to await the future lessons of experience; a reverence for the characteristic rights of freemen, and a regard for the public harmony, will sufficiently influence your deliberations on the question how far the former can be more impregnably fortified, or the latter be safely and advantageously promoted.

To the preceeding observations I have one to add, which will be most properly addressed to the House of Representatives. It concerns myself, and will therefore be as brief as possible. When I was first honoured with a call into the Service of my Country, then on the eve of an arduous struggle for its liberties, the light in which I contemplated my duty required that I should renounce every pecuniary compensation. From this resolution I have in no instance departed. And being still under the impressions which produced it, I must decline as inapplicable to myself, any share in the personal emoluments, which may be indispensably included in a permanent provision for the Executive Department; and must accordingly pray that the pecuniary estimates for the Station in which I am placed, may, during my continuance in it, be limited to such actual expenditures as the public good may be thought to require.

Having thus imported to you my sentiments, as they have been awakened by the occasion which brings us together, I shall take my present leave; but not without resorting once more to the benign parent of the human race, in humble supplication that since he has been pleased to favour the American people, with opportunities for deliberating in perfect tranquility, and dispositions for deciding with unparellelled unanimity on a form of Government, for the security of their Union, and the advancement of their happiness; so his divine blessing may be equally *conspicuous* in the enlarged views, the temperate consultations, and the wise measures on which the success of this Government must depend.

National Archives and Records Administration. (*This transcription was taken from the original document in the Records of the U.S. Senate, Record Group 46, in the National Archives.*)

2. Report on Manufactures, by Alexander Hamilton (1791)

As America's first secretary of the treasury, Alexander Hamilton presented this masterful report to Congress on December 15, 1791. It laid out economic principles for the industrialization of the new nation, including arguments for protective tariffs and the prohibition of imported goods manufactured elsewhere. These measures, he argued, would protect fledgling American industries.

The Secretary of the Treasury, in obedience to the order of the House of Representatives of the 15th day of January, 1790, has applied his attention, at as early a period as his other duties would permit, to the subject of manufactures, and particularly to the means of promoting such as will tend to render the United States independent of foreign nations for military and other essential supplies; and he thereupon respectfully submits the following report:

The expediency of encouraging manufactures in the United States, which was not long since deemed very questionable, appears at this time to be pretty generally admitted. The embarrassments which have obstructed the progress of our external trade, have led to serious reflections on the necessity of enlarging the sphere of our domestic commerce. The restrictive regulations, which, in foreign markets, abridge the vent of the increasing surplus of our agricultural produce, serve to beget an earnest desire that a more extensive demand for that surplus may be created at home; and the complete success which has rewarded manufacturing enterprise, in some valuable branches, conspiring with the promising symptoms which attend some less mature essays in others, justify a hope that the obstacles to the growth of this species of industry are less formidable than they were apprehended to be; and that it is not difficult to find, in its further extension, a full indemnification for any external disadvantages, which are or may be experienced, as well as an accession of resources, favorable to national independence and safety....

But the system which has been mentioned, is far from characterizing the general policy of nations. The prevalent one has been regulated by an opposite spirit. The consequence of it is, that the United States are, to a certain extent, in the situation of a country precluded from foreign commerce. They can, indeed, without difficulty, obtain from abroad the manufactured supplies of which they are in want; but they experience numerous and very injurious impediments to the emission and vent of their own commodities. Nor is this the case in reference to a single foreign nation only. The regulations of several countries, with which we have the most extensive intercourse, throw serious obstructions in the way of the principle staples of the United States.

In such a position of things the United States can not exchange with Europe on equal terms; and the want of reciprocity would render them the victim of a system which should induce them to confine their views to agriculture and refrain from manufactures. A constant and increasing necessity on their part for the commodities of Europe and only a partial and occasional demand for their own in return could not but expose them to a state of impoverishment, compared with the opulence to which their political and natural advantages authorize them to aspire. . . .

Not only the wealth, but the independence and security of a country, appear to be materially connected with the prosperity of manufactures. Every nation, with a view to those great objects, ought to endeavor to possess within itself all the essentials of national supply. These comprise the means of subsistence, habitation, clothing, and defense.

The possession of these is necessary to the perfection of the body politic; to the safety as well as to the welfare of the society. The want of either is the want of an important organ of political life and motion, and in the various crises which await a state it must severely feel the effects of any such deficiency. The extreme embarrassments of the United States during the late war from an incapacity of supplying themselves are still matter of keen recollection; a future war might be expected again to exemplify the mischiefs and dangers of a situation to which that incapacity is still in too great a degree applicable unless changed by timely and vigorous exertion. To effect this change as fast as shall be prudent merits all the attention and all the zeal of our public councils; 'tis the next great work to be accomplished.

Alexander Hamilton, *Report on Manufactures*, December 5, 1791 (Washington: Government Printing Office, 1913).

<small>BENJAMIN RUSH.</small> Image source: U.S. Library of Congress.
Artist Charles Balthazar Julien Fevret de Saint-Mémin.

3. BENJAMIN RUSH ON EDUCATION
IN THE NEW REPUBLIC

Dr. Benjamin Rush (1746–1813), one of the signers of the Declaration, was a leader and example of social reform in the early Republic, including his opposition to slavery and efforts at prison reform. The founder of the country's first Bible Society, Rush had a particular interest in education and here discusses the value of loyalty to country and public service.

The business of education has acquired a new complexion by the independence of our country. The form of government we have assumed, has created a new class of duties to every American. It becomes us, therefore, to examine our former habits upon this subject, and in laying the foundations for nurseries of wife and good men, to adapt our modes of teaching to the peculiar form of our government.

The first remark that I shall make upon this subject is, that an education in our own, is to be preferred to an education in a foreign country. The principle of patriotism stands in need of the reinforcement of prejudice, and it is well known that our strongest prejudices in favour of our country are formed in the first one and twenty years of our lives. The policy of the Lacedemonians is well worthy of our imitation. When Antipater demanded fifty of their children as hostages for the fulfillment of a distant engagement, those wise republicans refused to comply with his demand, but readily offered him double the number of their adult citizens, whose habits and prejudices could not be shaken by residing in a foreign country. Passing by, in this place, the advantages to the community from the early attachment of youth to the laws and constitution of their country, I shall only remark, that young men who have trodden the paths of science together, or have joined in the same sports, whether of swimming, scating, fishing, or hunting, generally feel, thro' life, such ties to each other, as add greatly to the obligations of mutual benevolence.

I conceive the education of our youth in this country to be peculiarly necessary in Pennsylvania, while our citizens are composed of the natives of so many different kingdoms in Europe. Our schools of learning, by producing one general, and uniform system of education, will render the mass of the people more homogeneous, and thereby fit them more easily for uniform and peaceable government. . . .

I am aware that I dissent from one of those paradoxical opinions with which modern times abound; and that it is improper to fill the minds of youth with religious prejudices of any kind, and that they should be left to choose their own principles, after they have arrived at an age in which they are capable of judging for themselves. Could we preserve the mind in childhood and youth a perfect blank, this plan of education would have more to recommend it; but this we know to be impossible. The human mind runs as naturally into principles it does after facts. It submits with difficulty to those restraints or partial discoveries which are imposed upon it in the infancy of reason. Hence the impatience of children to be informed upon all subjects that relate to the invisible world. But I beg leave to ask, why should we pursue a different plan of education with respect to religion, from that which we pursue in teaching the arts and sciences? Do we leave our youth to acquire systems of geography, philosophy, or politics, till they have arrived at an age in which they are capable of judging for themselves? We do not. I claim no more then for religion, than for the other sciences, and I add further, that if our youth are disposed after they are of age to think for themselves, a knowledge of one system, will be the best means of conducting them in a free enquiry into other systems of religion, just as an acquaintance with one system of philosophy is the best introduction to the study of all the other systems in the world.

Next to the duty which young men owe to their Creator, I wish to see a regard to their country, inculcated upon them. . . . The same duty is incumbent upon every citizen of a republic. Our country includes family, friends and property, and should be preferred to them all. Let our pupil be taught that he does not belong to himself, but that he is public property. Let him be taught to love his family, but let him be taught, at the same time, that he must forsake, and even forget them, when the welfare of his country requires it.

Benjamin Rush, *Essays, Literary, Moral and Philosophical* (Philadelphia: Bradford, 1798).

4. The First Inaugural Address of Thomas Jefferson, Delivered at Washington, D.C., March 4, 1801

When Chief Justice John Marshall administered the executive oath of office to Thomas Jefferson in 1801, it was the first time an inauguration was held in Washington, D.C. The outcome of the election had been hard fought, because Jefferson and Aaron Burr had tied in the electoral college. It took a special session of the House of Representatives, in a thirty-hour debate and balloting, to give Jefferson the win. Burr became vice president.

Friends And Fellow-citizens: Called upon to undertake the duties of the first executive office of our country, I avail myself of the presence of that portion of my fellow-citizens which is here assembled to express my grateful thanks for the favor with which they have been pleased to look toward me, to declare a sincere consciousness that the task is above my talents, and that I approach it with those anxious and awful presentiments which the greatness of the charge and the weakness of my powers so justly inspire. A rising nation, spread over a wide and fruitful land, traversing all the seas with the rich productions of their industry, engaged in commerce with nations who feel power and forget right, advancing rapidly to destinies beyond the reach of mortal eye—when I contemplate these transcendent objects, and see the honor, the happiness, and the hopes of this beloved country committed to the issue and the auspices of this day, I shrink from the contemplation, and humble myself before the magnitude of the undertaking. . . .

Sometimes it is said that man cannot be trusted with the government of himself. Can he, then, be trusted with the government of others? Or have we found angels in the forms of kings to govern him? Let history answer this question. . . .

Still one thing more, fellow-citizens—a wise and frugal Government, which shall restrain men from injuring one another, shall leave them otherwise free to regulate their own pursuits of industry and improvement, and shall not take from the mouth of labor the bread it has earned. This is the sum of good government, and this is necessary to close the circle of our felicities. . . .

Relying, then, on the patronage of your good-will, I advance with obedience to the work, ready to retire from it whenever you become sensible how much better choice it is in your power to make. And may that Infinite Power which rules the destinies of the universe lead our councils to what is best, and give them a favorable issue for your peace and prosperity.

Norman Foerster and William Whatley Pierson, eds., *American Ideals* (Houghton Mifflin Co., 1917).

NOAH WEBSTER. Image source: U.S. Library of Congress.
Steel engraving from a painting by A. Chappel.

5. NOAH WEBSTER'S ORATION ON THE ANNIVERSARY OF THE DECLARATION OF INDEPENDENCE

In this cautionary offering on the twenty-sixth anniversary of the Declaration, Noah Webster warns America about those who would advance their own interests through the political system and by pandering to the people, even seducing and deceiving them. As a corrective, Webster points us to the values and examples of the patriots who have gone before.

Nations, like individuals, may be misled by an ardent enthusiasm, which allures them from the standard of practical wisdom, and commits them to the guidance of visionary projectors. By fondly cherishing the opinion that they enjoy some superior advantages of knowledge, or local situation, the rulers of a state may lose the benefit of history and observation, the surest guides in political affairs; and delude themselves with the belief, that they have wisdom to elude or power to surmount the obstacles which have baffled the exertions of their predecessors. . . .

If Moses, with an uncommon portion of talents, seconded by divine aid, could not secure his institutions from neglect and corruption, what right have we to expect, that the labors of our lawgivers will be more successful? . . .

The passions of men being every where the same, and nearly the same proportion of men in every society, directing their views to preferment, we observe that, in all governments, the object and efforts are the same, but the direction of those efforts is varied, according to the form of government, and *always applied to those who have the disposal of honors and offices.* In a monarchy, office-seekers are courtiers, fawning about the ministers or heads of departments. . . . in a pure democracy, they are orators, who mount the rostrum, and harangue the populace, flattering their pride, and inflaming their passions. . . . in a representative republic, they are the *friends of the people,* who address themselves to the electors, with great pretensions to patriotism, with false-hoods, fair promises, and insidious arts. . . .

Whatever may be the form of government, therefore, corruption and misrepresentation find access to those who have the disposal of offices; by various means and different channels indeed, but proceeding primarily from demagogues and office-seekers, of bold designs and profligate principles.

It is said, however, that we have constitutions of government, or fundamental compacts, which proscribe abuses of power, by defining the exact limits of right and duty, and controlling both rulers and people. But how long will a constitutional barrier resist the assaults of faction? . . . When a magistrate becomes more popular than the constitution, he may "draw sin as it were with a cart-rope" in the work of extending his power over the instrument which was intended to restrain usurpation.* Whatever vanity and self-confidence may suggest, in favor of the restraints of a paper compact, all history and uniform experience evince, that against men who command the current of popular confidence, the best constitution has not the strength of a cobweb. The undisguised encroachments of power give the alarm and excite resistance. . . . but the approaches of despotism, under cover of popular favor, are insidious and often deceive the most discerning friends of a free government. . . .

To be a tyrant with any tolerable degree of safety, a man must be fully possessed of the confidence of the *people*. . . .

* Editor's Note: Webster is here quoting from Isaiah 5:18, a passage pronouncing woe upon the unjust and those who "call evil good, and good evil" (v. 20).

The open advocate of a strong government is subject to popular odium, his encroachments are eyed with jealousy, or resisted by force. But the hypocritical pretender to patriotism acquires, in the confidence of the people, a giant's force, and he may use it like a giant. The people, like artless females, are liable to be seduced, not by the men they hate or suspect, but by those they love. . . .

A republican government, in which the supreme power is created by choice, is unquestionably the most excellent form of government in theory. . . .

But although a republican government is admitted to be the best, and most congenial to our state of society, its innate perfections and unavoidable abuses, render it far less durable, than its enthusiastic admirers have supposed. This conclusion, drawn from experience, should silence the complaints of men, who look for more perfection in government than it is susceptible of receiving; it should allay the animosities and temper the discussions of our citizens; . . . . it should produce a more indulgent spirit towards the faults of men in power and the errors of private individuals.

The consideration, also, that the intended effects of a free government, are mostly defeated by an abuse of its privileges, should make us more solicitous to acquire a deep and correct knowledge of its true principles, and more vigilant in guarding against the impositions of designing men. . . . men who seek offices by fair promises, and flatter only to deceive. Most men are more willing to command than to obey. . . . and more men are desirous to obtain public favor, than are willing to deserve it, by severe study and laborious services. One truth, also, ought to be deeply impressed on the minds of freemen, that men of real worth are always the last to seek offices for themselves. . . . and the last to clamor against men of worth who possess them. . . .

Let the youth of our country, who were not spectators of the distresses of the war; but who have entered upon the stage of life in time to see the silver locks of the revolutionary patriots, and to witness the scars and the poverty of the war-worn soldier. . . . let these ponder the history and listen to the tale of their fathers' sufferings, and their country's danger. Let them read the animated and energetic addresses of the first American Congress, whose firmness and eloquence would have honored a Roman Senate . . . Let them early imbibe the manly and dignified sentiments of that illustrious council which pointed out the road to independence . . . Let them catch a portion of the patriotic flame . . . and by learning to revere the sentiments, may they be led to follow the example, of those venerable sages. . . . Let them review, in imagination, the heroic achievements of the American troops. . . . Let them see, at Bunker's hill, a few hardy farmers, twice repulsing the numerous, well-marshalled columns of the foe, and holding the issue of the contest in suspense. . . . Let them transport their imaginations to the hills of Bennington, the fields of Saratoga, the almost inaccessible cliffs of Stony Point, and the plains of Yorktown where the armies of America closed their triumphs; there let them admire the heroism of the citizen soldier, and catch the spirit of victory. Then let them cast their eyes upon a shattered army, retreating before a triumphant foe. . . . See the magnanimous WASHINGTON, almost deserted and driven to despair, rallying a small band of half-clothed, dispirited troops, whose naked feet, lacerated with the frost bound clods, stained the road with blood, as they marched to the victories of Trenton and Princeton! Let scenes like these lead them to compassionate the distresses of a half-famished soldiery, who suffered and bled to defend the blessings which we now enjoy, and whose services are yet unrewarded. And when our youth see a needy soldier, grown old in poverty, or the widows and orphans of soldiers, doomed to want by the loss of their protectors, and the depreciation of government paper, let them open the liberal hand of bounty, and by relieving their wants, still divide with them the burthens and the distresses of the revolution. Let them consider that upon them has devolved the task of defending and improving the rich inheritance, purchased by their fathers. Nor let them view this inheritance of National Freedom and Independence, as a fortune that is to be squandered away, in ease and riot, but as an estate to be preserved only by industry, toil and vigilance. Let them cast their eyes around upon the aged fathers of the land, whose declining strength calls for their support, and whose venerable years and wisdom demand their deference and respect. Let them view the fair daughters of America, whose blushing cheeks and modest deportment invite their friendship and protection; whose virtues they are to cherish and reward by their love and fidelity; and whose honor and happiness it is their duty to maintain inviolable. Let them learn to merit the esteem and affections of females of worth, whose rank in life depends much on the reputation of their husbands, and who therefore never fail to respect men of character, as much as they despise those who waste their lives in idleness, gaming and frivolous pursuits.

And let us pay the tribute of respect to the memory of the illustrious hero who led our armies in the field of victory, and the statesman who first presided over our national councils. Let us review the history of his life, to know his worth and learn to value his example and his services. Let us, with a solemn pleasure, visit his tomb; there to drop a tear of affection, and heave a fervent sigh, over departed greatness. . . . There let us pluck a sprig of the willow and the laurel that shade the ashes of a WASHINGTON, and bear it on our bosoms, to remind us of his amiable virtues, his distinguished achievements, and our irreparable loss! . . . . Then let us resume our stations in life, and animated by his illustrious example, cheerfully attend to the duties assigned us, of improving the advantages, secured to us by the toils of the revolution, and the acquisition of independence.

AFTERWORD

Patriotism means more than love for your country. It means love for what makes your country *your country*. For Americans, that's a long list. And many (certainly not all) of the things that make us Americans are captured in the foregoing passages. In some cases, in sharp relief. Other times, only in shadows. This collection is far from definitive, complete, exhaustive, or anything of the sort. At best, it's introductory. But look at what we value, for what we hope, and these selections should seem familiar and close despite their temporal distance from us.

Familiarity and proximity, however, are not enough. There are the questions of obligation and action. What claims, if any, do these texts make on us? What should we do in response?

Each of us must sort out those answers, but it seems readily apparent to us that if we profess any genuine affection for what makes our country *our country*, then that must matter in more than sentiment. A gush of emotion or a finely turned thought are well and good, but they are insubstantial and frankly devalue the real flesh-and-blood sacrifices of those who have gone on before. To *live* Americanly in our communities, in our states, in our nation seems basic. To hold American leaders to account for these standards seems necessary. To hold *ourselves* accountable seems fundamental.

If these texts represent ideas and past actions that compose the American soul, then to disregard them is to reduce our country to a mere political mechanism, and America is so much more than that.

INDEX

Index

John Hancock

Rob Morris   John Penn

Benjamin Rush   Wm Pac

Thos

Benj Franklin   Geo Taylor

Wm Floyd

Wm Hooper   Casar Ro

John Morton

Carter Braxton   Arthur Middlet

Francis Lightfoot Lee   George Wy

Geo Read   Rich ard Henry

Tho: M: Kean   Josiah Bartlett

Edward Rutlidge   Matthew

Ths Hayward Junr

Thomas Lynch Junr   Geo Clyme

Saml Adams   Jas Smith   W

Geo Walton   Lewis Morris   Ol